MORALS AND THE NEW THEOLOGY

MORALS AND THE NEW THEOLOGY

by

H. D. LEWIS

Professor of Philosophy
University College of North Wales, Bangor

"hating Pelagius over much."

ERASMUS

HARPER & BROS.
PUBLISHERS
NEW YORK

Printed in Great Britain

CONTENTS

CONTENTS

PREFACE

We are living to-day in an irreligious age, and that at a time when religion should matter supremely. For, as several thinkers have remarked of late, the crisis which seems to be deepening about us is an essentially religious one. If it can be brought to a successful issue, we may expect to pass shortly to a new period of civilization, one which will be marked, not merely by new attainments of a general kind, but also by a higher level of religious life and the deeper permeation of life as a whole by religion. On the other hand, religious stagnation may lead to overwhelming disaster. In these circumstances it does not augur well that religion is of such little concern to the average individual, least of all perhaps in the countries that used to constitute Christendom. The masses are strangers to the Churches, they have no religious equivalent, and the Bible is a closed book to them. Of those who remain within the Christian fold, a rapidly dwindling number, few have any deep convictions which could give reality to their religious observances and profession of belief. Religion matters least when it should matter most.

Religious leaders, often with the active support of bewildered politicians, have sought various remedies for this situation, ranging from crude publicity stunts to bold evangelical campaigns and measures for religious instruction in schools. None of these seem to have availed; nor do we feel in our hearts that we seriously expected them to do so. They have touched the fringes of the problem without ever cutting to its deeper levels. That can only be done when we ask, with far greater boldness than hitherto, how much of what is normally presented in the name of religion is entirely unacceptable to-day. The ordinary man is unmoved, and often contemptuous, because most that he associates with religion is at variance with his plainest convictions. And the fault, in this matter, does not lie with him. It lies with those who could have made bolder efforts to discover religious truths afresh at the level of our present attainment and cultural advances, a task *not* to be accomplished by attenuated presentations of religious realities in scientific or psychological terms. To lay real hold on religion, we must do so with our whole personality. But that is not possible as we have been taught to think of religion. And this, I believe, is the main reason for the drift from religion to-day.

This makes it all the more distressing that the theologians who seem most alive to the present plight of religion would have us go back to dogmatisms peculiarly out of place in our day. These may have a certain initial forcefulness and strong associations with great evangelical periods in the past. But we are also bound to ask *"Are they true?"* Barthianism has been hailed as a "preacher's theology." But that is a highly suspicious commendation. There can only be a spurious revival of religion unless our first concern is to find, not "a preacher's theology," but the *truth*.

To present these matters fully would require much space. The aim of the essay that follows is merely to give some examples of the main ways in which the dominant trend in Protestant theology to-day is altogether at variance with elementary ethical principles which we take for granted from day to day, and which the moral philosopher seeks to describe and correlate. Except at one or two points, as in Chapters III and IV, where it seemed unavoidable, technical matters have been excluded. This was in the ambitious hope that the book would be of interest, not only to the professional student of religion, but also to the layman, and to young students at our universities who, if they turn to religion at all, are apt to be inundated by reactionary "orthodox" doctrines, with the consequence that, when they are not wholly repelled, they come to have an extremely unhealthy religious life. If, in addition to registering its protest against the estrangement of religion from morality, this book should also suggest some points of departure for any who may undertake the comprehensive survey of the present relations of ethics and religious thought which we so urgently need, the author will be deeply gratified.

The title calls for some comment. For recently there has been a radical change in the use of the term "New Theology." From designating an adventurous liberalism which, with all its proneness to rationalize religion too completely, did at least hold to the aim of making religion comformable to reason, it has come to stand for a wholly reactionary dogmatism. In its new context, the term is not a happy one. But what it lacks in inherent suitability it may at least gain in exclamatory value. It is certainly less cumbersome than "New Protestantism," and less restricted than "Neo-Calvinism" and "Neo-Lutheranism." I have therefore ventured to follow Professor Charles Raven and others in retaining the term "New Theology" for that type of Protestant thought which predominates to-day, and which I wish to discuss.

It was unfortunate for me that the protracted illness of the present Head of the Department of Philosophy at Bangor, Professor James Jones, made it impossible to consult him about this book. But I am grateful to him for the generous interest which he has invariably taken in the private studies of members of his staff.

Acknowledgments are also due to several others. Firstly, to Professor C. A. Campbell of Glasgow. This is not the place to acknowledge my general indebtedness to Professor Campbell, but those who know him will realize how fortunate I have been in having had constant discussion with him of the main problems of religion and ethics, and especially of the problem of moral freedom about which he has written with such distinction. Professor Campbell read the whole of my manuscript, and Professor John MacMurray has also put me freshly and deeply in his debt in similar fashion. I have further to thank two theologians, Professor Leonard Hodgson and Dr. John Lowe of Christ Church, Oxford, both of whom were kind enough to read my book and send me many suggestions whose worth was not diminished by sharp disagreement with some of my views. I wish also to thank my brother-in-law, Mr. Aneurin Jones, for typing this book, and my wife for correcting the proofs and preparing an index.

H. D. LEWIS.

CHAPTER I

THE RIFT

IF SOMEONE WERE TO take up a philosophical book on ethics written in fairly recent times, it is not very likely that he would find anywhere within it the word 'sin.' 'Wrong-doing,' 'moral evil,' 'vice,' 'malevolence,' these and their synonyms he would often encounter, but not 'sin.' On the other hand, if he were to turn to a theological book and examine such parts of it as are concerned with moral evil and wrongdoing, 'sin' is the term he would meet most often and in the most crucial contexts. This difference of terminology is symptomatic of the unfortunate rift that is so noticeable to-day between the work of the theologian and the moral philosopher.

This essay has the main object of arousing concern at the deepening of this rift, and the discussion of particular problems, inevitably cursory from the number of matters on which it is hoped to touch, will, I trust, be viewed in the light of its subservience to this main purpose. There appears to me to be no more urgent matter in the field of theological study than to relate the main features of contemporary theology to what we feel bound to believe about the moral life, to bridge what appears at the moment an impassable gulf. Until this is achieved we cannot enter properly on the heritage of religious understanding and awareness which this generation seems otherwise destined to receive as the supreme compensation for the stresses and confusions through which it has passed. Something of the greatest significance and something whose import is finally religious seems to be preparing, and we have a foretaste of it in a burst of religious and theological thinking whose challenge and power few will deny, however much it may also bewilder us. But the title deeds that can make the gain properly ours will be incomplete if it cannot be made less repugnant to our reason, less starkly a reversal of the course of civilization in modern times, less obviously a surrender of the 'whole person' to a dualism which, however it be obscured at the start, cannot fail to be enervating and distracting, and, eventually, immensely tragic. The advance of religion to-day must be an advance of man in the fullness of his powers; otherwise it may leave him so disordered as to plunge him into far greater distress than that which it is his terrible lot to endure to-day.

It is not contended that the way for mankind will ever be smooth. God forbid that it should, for there is no real living where there is no tension. But there is a peculiar kind of tempest which it is the destiny of man to ride, and this is wholly different from the violent vortex in which he is liable to be engulfed, and lost altogether, when some aspect of religious life is deepened at the cost of enlightenment and regardless of violence to the moral self.

It has to be stressed that the rift which I have mentioned is much more distressing than a mere cooling of relations between workers in cognate but fairly independent fields. Our proneness to excessive specialization is rightly a subject of complaint to-day. The sciences have much to learn from one another, and science from the arts; a healthy civilization must maintain genuine contacts between different kinds of culture; it must not be too departmentalized if there is to be real enrichment of experience and a directing of our own destinies such as befits human beings; but the respective sciences have, none the less, their own provinces and each one proceeds to conclusions which do not require very direct support from other studies. The lack of co-operation between various disciplines does not, therefore, normally have any immediately drastic effect, even where those disciplines are cognate. But the matter is far otherwise in regard to the relation between theology and morals, for these are not just cognate studies, they are concerned in large part with precisely the same questions.

There are indeed questions which the theologian asks that are not directly the concern of the moralist. We do not examine the proofs of the existence of God in lectures on moral philosophy. Neither would such lectures normally have any reference to God or raise any question about his existence, his nature or his relation to man. This, as I shall argue below, is a perfectly proper procedure. The main ethical truths do not depend directly on religion, although the more specific or material problems of ethics require close account to be taken of religious aspirations. But theology is vitally concerned with the meaning of value and the nature of the values attainable in human life; it has to do especially with moral worth and its opposite, moral wickedness or sin. But it cannot be that these qualities have two natures, one which they present to the moralist and another which the theologian is privileged to view. Truth is one, and although the same object may be studied in different aspects, there can only be one proper answer to a particular question. It is in the measure that the questions they ask coincide that the divorce of theology from moral philosophy is most to be deplored.

The gravity of the situation is deepened by the indifference, one might almost say equanimity, with which it is accepted by both parties. There appears to subsist between them a kind of gentleman's agreement not to poach on each other's preserves. They are content, for the most part, to live and to let live. And this must be due, if not to a lack of seriousness of purpose—not, I am quite sure, the real explanation—to mutual ignorance and to contempt of a very profound kind. To many philosophers the theologian is apt to appear an innocent enthusiast who creates problems for himself and can be left to his foibles without serious hurt to himself or the community. The theologian, on the other hand, while he is more respectful to the philosopher, supposes that the problems of the latter are too abstract to have any special bearing on the more specific problems of religion. He is ready to quote the philosopher on occasion, but even this compliment is highly doubtful, for the fundamental irrelevance of the philosophical allusions is often evident in their inexactitude and lack of understanding.[1]

There are indeed notable exceptions. The late Professor A. E. Taylor and Professor C. C. J. Webb provide obvious examples. The practice of drawing a sharp distinction between the philosopher and the theologian has also been more common on the Continent and is less in harmony with our tradition. But of recent years there has been a proneness for English scholars and thinkers to be much affected by the same habit. And even if I seem to exaggerate the unconcern of the moral philosopher and the theologian in general in regard to the differences between them, it does not seem possible at all to question the extent to which the typical moral philosopher of to-day is proceeding on assumptions, and advancing conclusions, diametrically opposed to the main trend of contemporary theology. That is what I really wish to establish and to stress.

The situation is not without parallel in the past. The best thought of the latter half of the last century was embarrassed by a similar dualism. And in that case it seems certain that the philosophers were most at fault. Advancing mechanistic and mainly naturalistic views of

[1] See note to Chapter I, p. 17.

14

man, and looking to science to dissolve all problems in the magic crucible of evolution, they were at the same time reluctant to surrender the moral and religious faith in which they had been nurtured. They therefore struck on the happy idea of allowing, as T. H. Green puts it, their "deeper convictions . . . to take their chance alongside of seemingly incompatible scientific beliefs."[1] Idealism was largely an answer to the challenge of this stultifying dualism. And idealism tended to bridge the gulf, not merely by correcting the crudities of naturalistic philosophy, but also, in a pardonable excess of enthusiasm, by seeking to rationalize religion through and through. Our present quandary may be traced in part at any rate to this source. The religious thinker to-day is apt to regard the support he may derive from philosophical quarters as of doubtful value and too dearly bought. He dreads the peaceful penetration of the sympathetic philosopher more than the violent antagonism of the older materialist or the unbeliever. He wishes to be saved especially from his friends.

This, then, will help to explain the combination of coolness and contemptuous politeness which subsists between philosophers and theologians to-day. But the real root of the trouble must be sought further back. Since the Reformation the various disciplines have tended more and more to take an independent course, with the ideal of being self-sufficient. Indulging themselves to the limit in the freedom which they acquired in the sixteenth century, and knowing how much progress and enlightenment were retarded by the dominance of religious thought in earlier centuries, they have held it their main interest to resist the intrusion of the outsider. This was the perpetual vigilance with which they sought to guard their freedom. Nor was this peculiar to science

[1] *Prolegomena to Ethics*, Section 1.

and the strictly cultural activities. In every regard freedom has been largely thought of as the mere absence of restraint. States viewed their freedom in terms of absolute sovereignty and individuals thought of the goal of their freedom as the minimum of State interference and the extension of unrestricted competition. We have passed through the great centuries of individualism. But that chapter is closing now, closing in the stress and turmoil of two world wars. Such a period is fraught with the gravest dangers, and we have to be on our guard especially against over-simplification and reactionary excesses. But it is evident that the time has now come for a new synthesis in all the main departments of thought and action, a fusion of the main forces of civilization that will direct them to a higher stage. This is the background in the light of which the present plight of theology and philosophy can be properly understood. On the one hand there is the pride in their emancipation which has worked its way into the heart of all the main disciplines in modern times, reinforced by the need for specialization which the wider range of our knowledge and activities makes the more inevitable. And, again, arising out of this we have the proneness of a particular discipline, when new syntheses and extensions of its scope are required, to undertake this work on its own, to grow from within rather than fuse with elements from without. This is as noticeable in the relations of the various sciences to one another as in the relation of science as a whole to art and religion. Such growth is anæmic and unnatural, and there is created also a bewildering overlap, a curiously half-cultivated no-man's-land in which vague encounters take place and ill-shapen things appear—the paradoxes and blatant contradictions by which the ambitious specialist seeks to correct the limitations of his own resources, a proneness, very markedly evident in religion, to revel in unreason where a little breadth of vision and common sense would provide a simple solution.

And now that we know what we have to expect let us venture into this wild country and take a closer note of its character. In a brief survey the most that we can obtain is a glimpse of some of its main features.

NOTE

In connection with the proneness of some theologians to make rather hasty and ill-judged pronouncements about the views held by philosophers, consider the account that is given of the views of Hobbes and Rousseau in the chapter on 'Philosophers and Theologians' in Dr. N. Micklem's recent book, *The Theology of Politics*. The essay as a whole is very shrewd and informative; and its main thesis that "individualism leads directly to its apparent antithesis, the organic idea of the State and of society" (p. 43) seems to me to be very true and to afford a most important clue to the totalitarian ills that oppress us to-day. But the reader will hardly be helped to a right understanding by the facile simplification which tells of "the Communism of Rousseau and Karl Marx or the National Socialism of Hobbes or Adolf Hitler" (p. 53). To describe Hobbes as "the philosophic father of the totalitarian state, Rousseau of red revolution" (p. 41) is almost as much a darkening of counsel as the gibe which declares: "If Herr Hitler had read Hobbes's *Leviathan*, his often expressed admiration for the British would be more easily intelligible" (p. 38). This strange pronouncement is not qualified by any hint of Hobbes's most emphatic insistence that laws should be 'good lawes,' laws that are "Needful, for the good of the people, and with-all perspicuous" (*Leviathan*, Chapter XXX), that laws should be like hedges to keep the traveller in the way and not hinder him, that "the good of the Sovereign and People cannot be separated" (*op. cit.*, Chapter XXX), that the first law of Nature bids men seek peace and maintain it (*op. cit.*, Chapter XIV) and that to this end they should "*keep their covenants made*"—to mention only a few of the ways in which Hobbes, the rationalist, stands in the sharpest contrast to the fanatical aggressive Nazi. Again, to represent Rousseau as the idealizer of happy savages ("free and delightful beings . . . just, gentle, wise," p. 40) is simply to perpetuate the unscholarly habit of interpreting Rousseau in terms of his earlier works, and those which are most popularly known, to the neglect of his more mature books, the *Economie Politique* and the *Contrat Social*, and those significant portions of an early draft of the latter work, in which there is a long description of the natural man as a stupid and limited animal requiring society to make him moral and intelligent. Many strands have gone to the weaving of Rousseau's theories and his influence may be discerned in more directions than one, but we have barely got beyond the popular misinterpretations of the famous opening sentence of his *Contrat Social* in Dr. Micklem's affirmation that the closing words of the *Communist Manifesto*, "Proletarians have nothing to lose but their chains," is an echo of the 'naïve optimism' of Rousseau.

It may be that philosophers have been equally irresponsible in references to noted theologians. If so, it only underlines the necessity for closer contacts between them.

CHAPTER II

ETHICAL OBJECTIVITY AND RELIGION

A QUESTION THAT INVITES immediate discussion from anyone with our purpose before him is that of the status of moral philosophy itself. Are there distinctively ethical ideas which it is the special business of the moralist to examine? In one regard the moral philosophers and the theologians will be found in much agreement on this matter. They can agree in rejecting certain views out of hand. These are the naturalistic views which claim to find in the nature of man an adequate clue to the meaning of ethical ideas. As against all such views, whether they take the form of the 'scientific ethics' which our generation has not altogether discarded, or a fairly generous humanism, in which we must include idealism—so far as it cannot overcome its initial subjectivism—the moral philosopher and the theologian will often combine to-day in stressing the ultimacy and uniqueness of moral conceptions. Man is not 'the measure.' His duties are given him, they are claims which he must fulfil, claims which must, indeed, in some way be within his power, but which do not depend on his own reactions and impressions. His conscience claims to reveal to him the nature of these duties, but it is a fallible conscience, and while he must always set himself to do the best he can according to his lights, he can never be sure that his conduct is 'materially' or outwardly suitable to the situations in which he finds himself. The truth is not relative to us in ethics any more than in other spheres. Our duties exist in the nature of things, and there are independent standards which we presuppose in any appraisement of men's activities. This has been exhibited with consummate mastery by distinguished writers in recent years,[1] and although the principle itself is not altogether novel, there is such a grasp of its implications and skilfulness in the exposition of it as to mark a very substantial advance in moral philosophy—an advance which, incidentally, appears to me to prepare the way for such a treatment of final metaphysical problems as may enable the present century to signalize itself in the history of thought by its treatment of these ultimate problems, much though metaphysics may be out of fashion in some quarters. For that reason alone the progress made recently in moral philosophy should be better known. But society will also benefit very substantially in more immediate and practical ways by a vindication of the supremacy of conscience, especially in times of revolution and change.

Opposition to the present emphasis on the uniqueness and ultimacy of ethical ideas comes in the most formidable shape from those quarters where the social aspects of ethical principles are most jealously guarded. The individual, it will be admitted, is not 'the measure.' But what then? Is it not to society that we look to correct the limitations of our private opinions? The attractiveness of this view can readily be understood. For it carries with it a certain finality and security by which the individual is spared a great deal of effortful thinking and anxiety. He can surrender his conscience into the safe-keeping of his community. But in fact the resources of society in this matter are not inexhaustible. And when every allowance has been made for the deference we should pay to established opinions, and to the claims of important social institutions, the fact remains that society, like the individual, is fallible, and that the claims of its

---

[1] For example, by Professor G. E. Moore in *Principia Ethica* and *Ethics*, and by Sir David Ross in *The Right and the Good* and *The Foundations of Ethics*.

institutions have a limit—a limit which may, in some circumstances, justify open resistance. This is the rock on which the celebrated doctrine of the 'general will,' which had such a vogue in the last century, is finally wrecked. In any sense in which we could plausibly speak of a general will' of society, that 'will' has endorsed practices and institutions which we would not hesitate to condemn and oppose.[1]

It seems, then, that there is no final resting place for the consciences of men in the 'will of society.' To seek such easement of the burden of thinking for ourselves, not only takes away much of the adventurousness of the moral life, it also sets us well on the highroad that culminates in the ruthless oppression of totalitarianism. This has been fully exhibited in recent years. And although we shall have to return to some aspects of this problem later, little would be gained by repeating at this point the arguments which are so fully available to the reader in recent books on moral philosophy. I propose to take it as established that there are distinctive ethical principles which do not depend in any ultimate way on our own reactions and attitudes.

It does not, of course, follow that we have invariably a clear grasp of these principles. On the contrary, it is the postulation of standards independent of ourselves that makes honest doubt and the fallibility of ethical judgments intelligible. As a practical corollary, the more we appreciate the objectivity of ethical truth the greater the care with which we shall examine our own ethical convictions and those of others in the hope of attaining

---

[1] Readers of T. H. Green's *Principles of Political Obligation* will remember how difficult he found it to account for the rights of a monotheistic reformer in a community which worshipped many Gods, or the right of a slave to his freedom in a society which sanctioned slavery. See especially Lecture H on 'Has the citizen rights against the State?'

the closest conformity to ultimate standards that i
possible to us.[1]

So far, I believe, it will not be difficult for me to carr
theological thinkers with me. But when it is asked 'Wha
more is involved in the notion of an ultimate standard?'
there will be some rather sharp differences of opinion
and the expediency to which the theologian resorts a
this point is closely related to further principles tha
have a high place in theology to-day, and which appea
to me to take away from the advances made by ethical
writers the enlightenment on still more ultimate issues
which I believe they can give. As a result of these errors,
the theologian seems also very hard put to it to maintain
that ultimacy of moral principles and their independence
of social standards and private conviction which, at
first, he appears so ready to admit. He finds himself
dizzily swinging round in his tracks. This, I hope, will
be plain in due course.[2] The process begins as follows:

When it is urged that ethical standards do not depend,
in the final account, on the reactions or opinions of men,
the religious thinker is tempted to represent this conclusion
as a supreme example of man's dependence on God. The
idea of obligation cannot be derived from some analysis
of our nature. Ideals or duties stand over against us; as
demands they cannot be rooted in our own desires; indeed,
their independence is such that we can never be quite
certain of their content, a predicament which will require
consideration shortly. But in so far as our ideals are in
this way outside our own nature, does it not follow that
they are best described as demands that are made upon
us by God; is not the moral law the embodiment of His

[1] I have discussed the practical importance of the idea of moral
objectivity in my paper, 'Obedience to Conscience' (*Mind*, July, 1945).
[2] Cf. especially Chapters VIII and IX.

will for men; is not this the only way in which it can have ultimate authority, be a 'categorical imperative'? So, at least, the theologian will usually argue. And I would not wish to quarrel very seriously with him on this particular issue were it not related to another much more important matter where, I believe, traditional theology violates a most fundamental delivery of the moral consciousness.

The main point that I wish to make in direct comment upon the tendency to seek support for ethical principles in religious truths, and thereby also to consolidate the latter, is that the logic of the position is so far removed from the attitude we are bound to adopt in practice that it will confuse the ordinary man to the extent of seriously jeopardizing his religious beliefs or deferring his attainment of them. We never in practice adhere to the view of the relation of ethical truths to religious truths presupposed in the position in question. For that view would make it altogether unreasonable to believe that we have moral obligations and at the same time to fail to adopt a religious view of the world. If there is no God, then, on the present supposition, there is no moral obligation either. It might, of course, be replied that the connection between ethical principles and religious ones is not so evident to men as the reality of moral obligation. In this way it could be urged that all reasonably mature persons are aware of duties incumbent upon them, have elementary knowledge of right and wrong, but that they fail to take the further step and appreciate the implication of their ethical knowledge. But it does not seem to me that this line can be adopted at all if the relation between ethics and religion is such that our obligations must be thought to owe their obligatory character directly to their being imposed by God. The illogicality of the person who continues to regard himself as a responsible agent in spite of his lack of any religious belief would have to be far too colossal for us to make his attitude the justification of treating him as a responsible person.

In other words, the moral life of the average non-believer would be based, not on genuine awareness of obligations but on delusions, on grounds which a little reflection would show to be wholly inadequate. But in fact we never adopt such an attitude. We put the "un-believer" on the same level in respect of moral account-ability as any other person. There may be certain ways in which the religious person is better placed to understand the content of ethical standards—I should certainly argue that there are—but we have not to enquire into the religious antecedents of a person's actions and ascertain his religious beliefs, or lack of beliefs, before we credit him with an understanding of the nature of right and wrong and an awareness of elementary duties. Neither do we hold for a moment that in acknowledging such duties the ordinary person, if he is not also religious, is just deluding himself or acting on ideas which he has acquired from others to whom religion was real and important, a kind of survival from the environment in which he was nurtured but for which there is no genuine foundation in his own experience.

The view that we really adopt is that mature persons have a proper awareness of moral distinctions quite independently of their adoption of any religious faith. There are many difficulties attaching to religious truths which do not affect ethical truths, and while fully ready to acknowledge these difficulties as a genuine explanation of the absence of religious belief, and, therefore, of the specifically religious practice, we do not for a moment treat a repudiation of moral responsibility with the same forbearance. And this is simply because fundamental ethical knowledge is such that it presents itself directly to the mature person quite independently of more

omplicated matters of religious belief. It presents itself
o us in the same way as other principles on which we
xpect the normal sane person to act whether he holds a
religious belief or not. The fundamental ideas of ethics,
n other words, have a finality and self-sufficiency not
fundamentally different from the principles of arithmetic.
They are not to be derived from any analysis of our own
nature, but neither are they to be derived from religion.
Their objectivity consists in their commending themselves
independently of any support extraneous to themselves.

When this conclusion is disputed, as it often is by
religious thinkers, I believe we ought to apply a very
simple test. This would consist in supposing that there is
no reality other than the events which make up the life
of man in the present world. Even the most devout should
not find it very hard to make this supposition, for it is a
belief that is actually held by many more persons than
those who profess any profound religious convictions
in Western countries to-day. There is nothing blatantly
contradictory about it, no palpable absurdity. In that
case we may suppose for a moment that the unbeliever is
right. But would it not still be true that we ought to treat
our neighbour in one way rather than another? Should
we not still succour the needy, alleviate pain and avoid
the infliction of it, seek a fair distribution of material
goods, cultivate our talents, and generally so conduct
ourselves that the fleeting spell of man's life on earth
should be as full of richness and wonder and the glow of
affection as it is possible for it to be? Admitting, as the
present writer is most ready to admit, that life would be
full of frustration and lack the only salve that will bring
genuine easement to the mind of man, it would still be
true, to limit ourselves to the obvious, that cruelty would
merit condemnation and kindness praise. Indeed, these
virtues and vices might reveal their nature all the more

clearly in the glow of a purely secular light. And may not the understanding acquired in this way prove in the end a means of enrichment and sanity in the religious life itself?

One understands the enthusiasm which prompts the advocate of religion to seek in the solid and not easily disputed facts of the moral life a firm foundation for the more intangible truths of religion. But his impatience may often prove his undoing. This is not merely for the reason already intimated, namely that religion is made to rest on what is so palpably a misconception that it will hardly commend itself to any not already disposed for other reasons to accept religious views, and approaching the problem in a very partisan spirit. There is also the need for genuine ethical objectivity as an indispensable element in a religious view of the world. Although ethical truths require no direct support from religion, except in so far as we have some specifically religious duties like acts of worship in mind, there can be no adequate presentation of religious principles that does not make a very fundamental use of ethical objectivity. It is not implied here that the existence of God can be known as an immediate postulate of the moral law, although that is in no way ruled out by our insistence that ethical truth is independent of religion. As Dr. Ewing puts it: "I conclude that ethics cannot be derived from theology, but must rather come first. It does not follow that it may not serve as the basis of an argument for the existence of God."[1] It is, I believe, the plausible, but not, it seems to me, finally tenable belief that an argument of this kind is possible, coupled with a vague notion—for which coherence theories of truth are partly responsible—that the distinction of premise and conclusion in an argument is not ultimate, that accounts in many cases for the

[1] "Ethics and Belief in God," *Hibbert Journal*, Vol. XXXIX, p. 357.

stubbornness of a view so contradictory of our best thought and practice as that ethical truths have no validity apart from religion. But, to return to the main point, while it does not seem to me possible to base an argument for the existence of God on the moral law alone, I am persuaded that ethical truths constitute indispensable elements in the kind of consideration by which the main truths of religion are established. To show how they can be so established would take us far afield and require consideration of many matters which cannot be brought within the limits of this discussion. But if the present view is the true one, then it will also be seen that the theologian who presses too eagerly for a transformation of ethical principles into immediate religious truths is depriving himself of the real and indispensable contribution of ethics to theology; he invalidates evidence on which he must draw. And it is for this reason, as well as for the effect on the possible convert of the presentation of religious views on grounds so open to criticism, that I accuse the kind of theologian we have been discussing of allowing his enthusiasm to defeat his real purpose.

To eliminate misunderstanding at this point it has to be stressed that my view of the relation of ethics to religion does not seem to me in any way tantamount to a denial of the absolute or unlimited nature of God. For I do not wish to claim for ethics any independence not accorded to other truths that commend themselves in and for themselves to the mind of man. In so far as all truths can be shown ultimately to lead to religious truth, and I, for one, believe that this is the case, then ethics also depends on religion. But this dependence is of a very special kind, and I am sure that we are not representing it in the proper way when we suppose that the idea of obligation, and its content, is only meaningful for us as an immediate command of God. There are issues here also which, in addition to their very considerable difficulty, would require much space to consider adequately; and among them the sense in which we are to think of the omnipotence and perfection of God constitutes a problem upon which no one should venture to comment in any but the most guarded terms. But the very difficulty of the problem, while precluding further comment upon it here, reinforces our insistence that the ultimate dependence of reality, as apprehended by finite minds, upon the nature of God, is such as to preclude that specification of the nature of this dependence as is involved in relating one aspect of reality to the will of God in a way wholly different from the relation of dependence in which other finite realities stand.

This, then, is the point to be stressed. Whatever be the final metaphysical significance of ethics, the independence of ethical principles on any further metaphysical or religious questions is such that the meaning of ethical principles and their content can be understood by rational creatures with sufficient completeness to make them morally responsible quite independently of their apprehension of religious truths. No doubt, as we shall stress again, the general sensitivity of the religious mind usually enables it to appreciate finer shades of ethical distinctions. But even in these cases the truths discerned have no specific dependence on religion—except, of course, in the case of particular religious duties.

Where this is persistently denied there seems to be room for the suspicion that the theologian shares with his main antagonist, the naturalist, an unwillingness to acknowledge the distinctive character of duty which his rebuttal of naturalistic theories seems at first sight to involve. And that is, I believe, at the heart of a much more serious estrangement from the moral philosopher which we may now proceed to consider.

CHAPTER III

MORAL AUTONOMY AND FREEDOM

THE DEVIATION OF THE theologian from the position which normally commends itself to the moralist in regard to the inter-relations of their respective studies, as we have examined it hitherto, will not cause serious concern to the moral philosopher. For the assertion that ethical objectivity has a special foundation in religion will not in itself affect very materially the work of the moral philosopher in giving an account of the moral life in terms of ultimate objective principles. That is, if theologians or religious philosophers care to make these further assertions about ethical principles, the moralist might be well content to leave them to their problems—if the matter rested there. As it happens, it does not by any means rest there in modern theology. It is the beginning of heresies which affect very directly and deeply the central problems of moral philosophy itself.

For the ascription of the alien categorical character of ethical demands directly to their origin in the will of God carries with it also, as a rule, the curious but very persistent belief that these demands are so foreign to our nature that we cannot in any measure yield them of our own volition but only in so far as the power to obey is also given us by God. Indeed it is frankly asserted that obligation is not obligation proper unless it is alien in *both* these senses. This is a remarkably paradoxical position to adopt but it is made altogether central to the argument of some of the most influential books on theology in recent years. The following quotation, taken from a

writer who is considered a good example of the more
moderate of the Continental theologians, could be capped
by even more confident declarations in the same vein from
numerous other writers. This is how Brunner puts the
matter tersely and boldly for us:

"Duty and genuine goodness are mutually exclusive.
Obedience due to a sense of unwilling constraint is
bondage, and indeed the bondage of sin. If I feel I *ought*
to do right, it is a sign that I cannot do it. If I could
really do it, there would be no question of 'ought' about it
at all. The sense of 'ought' shows me the Good at
an infinite impassable distance from my will. Willing
obedience is never the fruit of a sense of 'ought' but only
of love. This is the paradox: that the sense of 'ought,'
through which alone I learn at all what freedom is in
this sense of 'ought,' unveils to me my formal freedom—
announces to me that I am in bondage to sin."[1]

Now, if this merely meant that there is a very wide
gulf between the 'dutiful will' and the 'holy will,' if it
were the purpose of Brunner merely to bring out a certain
transcendence of the moral standpoint that is involved
in religious union with God, then his statement would
have the highest importance; *in that context* his contention
could be readily endorsed, notwithstanding very fundamental problems that would remain to be considered.
But this is clearly not the way in which Brunner intends
us to understand his view. As presented by him the
position becomes a virtual a-moralism which simply
disregards the most elementary ethical postulates.

It is grossly misleading to describe obedience to our
duty as "due to a sense of unwilling constraint," and leave
the matter there. But what is more astonishing is the
calm assurance with which the freedom which we
normally associate with the idea of obligation is straight-

[1] *The Divine Imperative*, p. 74.

ay identified with bondage to sin, a paradox which rushes aside without the slightest ceremony what appears o be as deeprooted an assurance of the moral consciousness s any, namely that the 'sense of ought' carries with it he assumption that I can, not that I cannot. The solution of the problem of freedom is probably the hardest task hat confronts the moral philosopher. But the acrobatics by which ethical thinking is just made to stand on its head in the above quotation calls for a suppleness which he is not likely to acquire—not at any rate until he leaves he more sober tasks to which he is accustomed for a pell of really intensive training in the theological schools.

Brunner is not unaware of doing much violence to our ordinary ethical beliefs. But that does not daunt him. For he includes in his condemnation of 'philosophical ethics' a complete repudiation of any ethical thinking that is *sui generis* and distinctive. This is the "short way" that the theologian is, apparently, privileged to take with the dissenting moralist. Ethics is to be just a part of the immediate exposition of the specifically religious aspect of experience. If, therefore, there should appear to be any contradiction between the requirements of ordinary ethical thinking and religious thinking, there is no question of suspending judgment, of asking, for example, whether the contradiction is really solvable in finite terms. Instead we have a distortion of ethical ideas to fit them immediately into a religious setting where alone they have place; and this leads to much more extravagant and unacceptable paradoxes than the admission of a fundamental incompatibility of ethics and religious thinking—should that prove the point at which we must rest. I do not say that it is.

The main force of Brunner's attack on 'philosophical ethics' is directed against Kant. There are, according to Brunner, 'two great systems' that confront one another in the 'philosophical ethic,'[1] Naturalism and Idealism.[2] The former he describes quite properly as "an attempt to explain the moral life from natural facts"; and we have already fully endorsed the rejection of this kind of ethics. This is one point at which a moralist may stand very firmly with the theologian. The second system is the 'ethic of duty for duty's sake.' This is the principle especially enunciated by Kant, and while there is much in the moral and metaphysical theories of Kant which does not seem to be properly presented by Brunner, and some important respects in which he and his fellow theologians seem not to have availed themselves of the most important advances in Kantian scholarship, yet he shows true discernment in selecting Kant as his real opponent. For Kant is the thinker above all others who gave prominence to those particular ethical principles which, while they seem to be such clear deliveries of the moral consciousness, are very disconcerting to traditional theology. It will therefore be instructive to consider more closely the points at issue between Brunner and Kant.

The doctrine upon which Brunner fastens especially is that of the autonomy of the moral law. And we have first to emphasize that the interpretation of this principle by Kant himself varies from one reference to another. This has been a source of much confusion to his followers as well as to his critics. There is therefore particular

[1] 'Philosophical ethics' is defined as "the attempt to base morality upon the human reason itself" (*op. cit.*, p. 35). As the term is intended to cover, among others, the theories of Plato and Socrates and modern utilitarians, as well as the ethics of Kant, the adequacy of the definition is highly questionable.

[2] To philosophers this term suggests the view that 'the real is the rational' in the sense intended by Hegel or Bradley. In ethics it stands for the view of the moral good as fulfilment of the self. But in the present context it is used for the ethic of 'duty for duty's sake.' This will not be seriously misleading, since it is quite plain how the term is used by Brunner.

need to consider very carefully the meaning we give to this conception, and, if we are to level any particular criticism against Kant himself, to make it quite clear which possible meanings of the idea of autonomy we have in mind. I fear that there is little evidence of this kind of caution in the theological writings of which I complain.

We shall clarify the issue, I believe, if we distinguish three main meanings that can be attached to the autonomy of the moral law, although we cannot here consider in any careful fashion which is the most important for Kant and how they are related in his system as a whole.

The first meaning is that in which the moral law is not to be derived in any way from a natural impulse or tendency. It is, in other words, strictly a law, a requirement, not a mere 'end' derived from our own nature. It does not matter here that Kant had a very inadequate view of the natural desires and tendencies of man in as much as he accepted the kind of mechanistic and hedonistic view of desire which we find in Hume and in later thinkers like Bain and Mill. For even if we follow the idealist, as I think we must here, in applying the best principles of Kant's analysis of experience to the desiring side of our nature, and, thereby, arrive at a much more adequate view of it, the fact still remains that duty is a conception that presents itself to us independently of a natural impulse or inclination. Nor is the content of obligation to be derived from an analysis of any particular reaction of our own—as has been stressed above. In the idea of duty we have a distinctive ethical truth revealed, according to Kant, to man's practical reason.

Here then is one meaning of moral 'autonomy.' It can be identified, in essentials, with the claim we have made for ethical objectivity.

A second meaning is harder to describe. Keeping to essentials it is that duty must be freely fulfilled, it must be accepted because of its obligatory character and, therefore, independently of any natural urge to act as it requires. It must be duty for duty's sake, and this principle presupposes freedom in a way that is quite distinctive. Unfortunately Kant laid himself especially open to criticism at this point. For while he perceived, as no one seems to have perceived before him, that the 'morality of duty' becomes meaningful only on the basis of a conflict between inclination and duty, at least so far as to allow of the possibility of yielding to inclination rather than duty, yet his general metaphysical view led to such a separation of the rational side of our nature, by which the claims of duty are discerned, from the natural desiring side—in technical terms, of the pure from the empirical self—that the possibility of any conflict between them appears to be ruled out. The pure self is conceived in such a way that it invariably directs itself to what is obligatory, and the empirical self follows the course of natural desires. This dualism complicates the ethics of Kant in very serious ways—as commentators have pointed out very fully. It leaves the impression that the pure self, which is also the free self, is by its very nature responsive to duty, and this feature of Kantian ethics does lend some justification to the supposition that an ethics of duty such as he advances involves the notion of some inevitable obedience to law. But even if we had to leave the matter there without qualification it would still be very far from reasonable to regard this 'bondage to the law,' assuming that the terms are at all applicable, as bondage to sin. For it is by no means apparent how the mere fact of being constrained by the constitution of the self is *ipso facto* some kind of *sinful* bondage. The most that we could say is that this bondage is morally neutral. But it is much more important to add, as against the critics of Kant, that, while some features of his general philosophical position led him to the dualism which has the unfortunate consequences indicated, what Kant was struggling to fit into his system was the conviction which he considered, and I think very rightly considered, to be axiomatic in moral thinking—namely, that the idea of obligation involves the freedom of choice. This is the real and fundamental significance of the maxim which in due course became so celebrated, 'I ought, therefore I can.' There are, it must be admitted, some recent studies of Kant which do not make the meaning we have given to this maxim the fundamental one for Kant, but I believe it not very difficult to show that they are mistaken, notwithstanding the subtlety which occasionally marks them.[1]

This brings us to the third meaning of autonomy. If we are to hold fast to the maxim 'I ought, therefore I can,' especially on the interpretation which has just been given as the proper one, and one which, I must add, appears easily the first that would occur to us, then it seems also to follow that an agent cannot have a duty without being aware of that duty. I cannot be under any obligation to do what I do not perceive to be my duty if the ability to discharge a duty is essential to its being a duty. Duty must therefore be 'self-imposed' in the sense that I accept or recognize it.

Now this position, unavoidable and very elementary though it appears, is fraught with some considerable difficulties. For it appears, in point of fact, that we often have duties of which we are not aware. Indeed, in so far as we are never certain of our facts in the various situations in which we have to act, and in so far also as there is much defectiveness in our properly moral judgment, we can rarely if ever be certain what is our duty.

[1] Among the ablest of such attempts in recent years is *Morality and Freedom in Kant*, by W. T. Jones.

And this at first seems to lead to the curious consequence that we can never do our duty—just because we do not properly know it.

For this curious predicament recent ethics has a simple solution in the sharpness with which it draws the distinction—not altogether a new one—between the subjective and the objective senses of duty. The subjective duty is that duty that appears so to some particular person, and a man can be said to have done his duty in the sense that really matters so far as his moral worth is concerned if he is loyal to his own moral end or ideal. The objective duty is the course of action which he would consider his duty if he understood aright, the duty that we have in mind when we say that some honest or well-meaning person has done what is wrong. Unless we postulate this subsidiary meaning of duty, moral perplexity and disagreement about ethical problems become altogether inexplicable. There is clearly a sense in which a conscientious person can do what is wrong, although the matter is not very easily put into unambiguous terms.

Now the need for distinctions of this kind did not force themselves on Kant's notice. And this, I believe, is not very difficult to understand, although they are distinctions specially required by his principle of 'duty for duty's sake.' For Kant seems to have considered it much more important to vindicate the claims of morality in general, to rescue ethical ideas, and, in particular, the idea of obligation, from a scepticism to which much in the progress of thought in his day gave support. He was therefore never very seriously perturbed by the more specific problem of moral perplexity, and he does not seem to have been at all acutely aware of the fact that the content of duty might remain obscure after the idea of duty had been vindicated and allegiance to it assured. Indeed, he is apt to give the impression of supposing that the content of duty can be derived from the idea of duty itself. How far this was really his intention is not easy to ascertain, and scholars are debating the issue with some liveliness at the present time. But it seems quite clear that Kant did not seriously consider the difficulty raised for his theory by the fact of moral perplexity. And it seems also clear that this is closely bound up with his assumption that our duties could be laid out in very simple rules, among the most important of them being duties, such as telling the truth, which were of 'perfect obligation,' that is, duties which did not allow of any exception whatever the circumstances.

This is the aspect of Kantian ethics on which theological critics fasten with especial grimness. And since there is little in the writings of Kant himself to suggest the solution indicated above, but rather the impression of an attempt to proceed without the distinctions described, the conclusion is drawn that the ethics of Kant precludes any adequate treatment of the problem of the content of moral obligation, that it requires us to choose between the alternatives of seeking to deduce the content of duty from the idea of duty, an altogether impossible venture, or of offering an ethic of renunciation, of complete turning away from the world and its practical problems.[1] Had it been admitted that there is a meaning of duty in respect of which we may be mistaken about our duty, it would then be possible to proceed with an account of such ways as we have of arriving at those ideas about the content of our duty as seem the most likely to be true. But when this alternative is ignored, or not discovered—and there is no excuse for not discovering it to-day—

[1] Brunner thinks that this is the alternative which it would be more consistent for Kant to adopt. "Actually Kant should have moved forward to an ascetic ethic of absolute renunciation of the world," op. cit., p. 48.

37

the conclusion is drawn that the ethics of Kant presupposes a demand which can never be met,[1] and which a little reflection shows to be absurd, the demand namely that the content of duty should be invariably plain to any who are seriously anxious to ascertain it. In this way a critic such as Brunner argues that the 'ethics of obligation,' as ordinarily understood, must be discarded. In its stead he presents us with an account of sinfulness, and consequent guilt, that does not presuppose awareness of the wrongdoing in which it consists. Autonomy in the third sense we distinguished above goes thus by the board. This prepares the way for its rejection in the second sense. For if it is not necessary that we should know the evil that we do, it cannot be necessary either that we should be free to choose to do or not to do it. Finally, as the breakdown of the idea of autonomy in these two senses is equated with the failure to show that the idea of duty guarantees for the individual the knowledge of a content of duty which would make it meaningful, so also the

---

[1] It has to be admitted that philosophers have not always been averse from exploiting this paradox. The most notable example in recent years is that of the late Professor de Burgh. The nerve of his argument is presented in a paper on "Right and Good" (*Philosophy*, Vol. V, pp. 582-3) where he writes: "we can never know, in any particular situation what it is really right to do. We know indeed that it is always right, really and absolutely right, to do what we believe to be right. . . . But this knowledge is purely formal and gives no clue to the matter of moral obligation. Our beliefs and judgments as to material rightness . . . are notoriously liable to error. . . . We never get beyond what we, or other persons, judge to be right. . . . Once again, to put the paradox in its most glaring form, if we are never able to know our duty how can we perform it? And if we are never able to perform it, what meaning is there in calling it our duty?" Morality depends on the command to will "what can neither be willed nor known," it is the "endeavour to achieve the impossible." This paradox, for which, as we have urged, there is a simple solution, is made to bear the weight of the elaborate metaphysical view presented in the volume of Gifford Lectures, *From Morality to Religion*.

absence of this, or any other, infallible way of prescribing this content of duty is assumed to be sufficient reason for concluding that there is no such distinctive objective ethical truth which we can strive to ascertain by the exercise of any faculty which naturally belongs to us as human beings. As so often happens in other contexts also, objectivity is thought to require subjective certainty. Almost the reverse of this is the case in fact, for it is our uncertainty that makes us most conscious of a standard that is not dependent on ourselves. But it can be seen how 'autonomy' in the first of the senses noted above is wrecked on the same misconception about the implications of objective duty which proved so disastrous to the other senses of the term.

This helps the position in a further way. From ethics, as we noted, Brunner turns to religion; the moral life is only to be understood in terms of the demands which God makes upon the beings he has created. And just as there is no specific faculty by which man can become aware of these demands other than the revelation vouchsafed to him by God, so there are no specific ethical principles to which we may appeal against aspersions of guilt and sinfulness which we are presumed to incur because we fail to conform to such demands as have not been made plain to us in those revelations we have been fortunate enough to receive. In other words, since the rejection of the ethics of duty is bound up with the rejection of a distinctive ethical truth, there is little to hinder the presentation, under the guise of religious truths, of pseudo-ethical ideas which ethics, if its pronouncements were less suspect, would induce us to discard.

We see then how the general failure to appreciate the uniqueness and ultimacy of ethical truth is closely bound up with the rejection of the distinctively ethical requirements of individual responsibility and freedom of choice.

And herein, I believe, lies the significance of the particular opposition which Brunner shows to the Kantian idea of the autonomy of the moral law. It shows us how easy is the transition from the position that "The Good is simply and solely the will of God"[1] to the view that "The true Good lies only in the power of God and not in that of man; that no other human goodness and good conduct exists save that which is based on the free gift of God."[2]

At the core of this position is the assumption that sin is essentially ethical blindness. What we have is a Socratic ethic into which there have been infused ideas of guilt and responsibility altogether incompatible with such an ethic. As Brunner quite roundly states: "if man could see evil as it is, he would not be really evil."[3] Man is evil to the extent that God has not enlightened him.

This, it may be thought, is a very extravagant theology such as would only be possible to-day in countries where men have lost their intellectual balance in the stress of tragic and confused events. But the truth of the matter is that the uncompromising Continental theologians, while drawing support from profound religious experience which they have not yet fully understood, are carrying out with ruthless consistency assumptions which are deeply embedded in traditional theology, however much they may be disguised by vague formulations and uncertain concessions.

This needs to be stressed, and we shall therefore deviate a little from our main course to take up this topic in the next chapter.

[1] *Op. cit.*, p. 75.   [2] *Op. cit.*, p. 58.
[3] *Op. cit.*, p. 75.

CHAPTER IV

A CONCESSION

Many attempts have been made to combine the notion of a 'marred' or sinful human nature with the principle that responsibility involves individual choice. Traditionalist doctrines have often sought to make room for both conceptions. A common procedure, especially of late, is to describe the apparent contradiction between the view that man is the author of his sin and the view that he cannot help it, as a 'tension,' the suggestion being, if I understand right, that the contradiction can be resolved, but that in the circumstances of our finite life, or at least at the present stage of our growth, it must remain. This is a dangerous expedient, and it must be allowed that it is with reluctance that theologians take up this view. If it can be shown that there is no reason to believe in 'the sin we cannot help,' as I think is the case,[1] our position will be much more satisfactory. Other theologians seek to relieve the 'tension' by speaking of two kinds of sin or of two elements in the nature of sin, that which we can help and that which is inevitable. They persuade themselves thus that they meet the requirements of the moral consciousness, and thereby avoid the rigours of Brunner's teaching or the violent denunciation of human endeavour by Barth and his stricter followers, without inconsistency and without surrendering the essentials of the traditionalist doctrine. This position has attractions for a great many, and it draws on conceptions that have a high theological ancestry. But it does not in fact seem possible to work out a satisfactory view of the relation between the two types

[1] See below, Chapters VI and XI.

of sin or to bring the theory in general into accord with fundamental ethical principles. The failure of the attempt serves to deepen the impression that Brunner and his school are only working out with ruthless consistency the implications of the main traditionalist position.

We cannot go exhaustively into a subject of this kind in a brief discussion, but some study of a typical view will help to show that the strictures to be passed in later chapters on the more extreme positions which we shall be considering are not without relevance to the main tradition in Christian theology.

A very clear impression of the position to which I refer may be obtained from a recent volume by the late Professor O. C. Quick, entitled *The Gospel of the New World.*

Quick is very insistent that moral evil, and, indeed, as we shall also have occasion to note, all forms of evil, are due to an abuse of his freedom by the finite creature. To put it in his own words, "the ultimate source of evil in the world is the free act of the finite and created will which uses its freedom to do wrong and to disobey the will of God."[1] The freedom which man thus abuses is bestowed upon him, as we are also told, by a "mysterious self-limitation of the Creator"[2] in order that man may "of his own free will surrender himself."[3] That surrender is only possible where there is also "a capacity to choose and do wrong."[4] So we appear to have the fullest and most unambiguous acknowledgment of the demand of the moral consciousness that responsibility and freedom must go together.

Quick furthermore rejects Brunner's doctrine of the fall precisely because it represents man as a creature who has now "become powerless to do anything but sin."[5]

[1] *Op. cit.,* p. 31.   [2] *Op. cit.,* p. 37.
[3] *Op. cit.,* p. 37.   [4] *Op. cit.,* p. 37.
[5] *Op. cit.,* p. 35.

He is also quite emphatic that "the power of conscious choice resides in the individual man, not in the group, society, race, or nation,"[1] thus apparently dissociating himself from the idea of a collective responsibility which is so marked a feature of Continental theology. "It is the individual who is the bearer of God's image"[2] by his exercise of purposive control and choice.

So far the position is plain. But we are also told that a wrong choice in the past confuses our insight into ethical matters on subsequent occasions and thereby makes it impossible for us to discharge our duty fully. Sin in this way perpetuates itself. Once the wrongful choice has been made, "sin with all its dire consequences of corruption has gained a foothold in human nature; and the consequences are transmitted to every soul that is naturally born. Henceforth man's nature is marred."[3] "The responsibility of man, which is his initial freedom, becomes not only a burden but a bondage. For now he has to choose without clear insight to guide his choice; he has asserted his independence, forfeited the immediate constancy of God's help, and the greater the range of choice he wins, the greater the anxiety to which he is a prey."[4] "Fallen and unredeemed," he is "dogged by the conflicting moods of self-assertion and fear," and "he seeks to avoid the latter by further self-assertion."[5] In short, "Kant's doctrine about the autonomy of the will, though it expresses a profound truth about human nature as originally created, takes no account of the fall."[6]

It is not very clear what is meant by the "fall." It is not maintained that "Adam must have been a single individual as Christ was."[7] The fall "can only be described in terms of myth or speculation not historically verifiable,"

[1] *Op. cit.*, p. 36. [2] *Op. cit.*, p. 36.
[3] *Op. cit.*, p. 39. [4] *Op. cit.*, p. 40.
[5] *Op. cit.*, p. 40. [6] *Op. cit.*, p. 42.
[7] *Op. cit.*, p. 43, note A.

but there is evidence of it "in our present experience of its results," and we have therefore to regard it as "an historical event."[1] The most that is plain is that sin is thought to perpetuate itself by distorting our vision and depriving us of the help of God.

There are two matters here that require to be distinguished. Firstly, the blindness which sin induces and, secondly, the weakening of the will which is also the result of past sin. But it is not clear how Quick conceives the relation between these two. It is the first that he has mainly in mind, and it is not at all certain that he regards the weakening of the will as a further and independent factor in the corruption of human nature. His view invites the following comments.

Firstly, it can be very readily admitted that deliberate wrongdoing has an ill effect on our ethical judgment. Conscience, like other faculties, requires to be cultivated, and it can hardly be cultivated where there is no serious intention of minding its behests. There appears, indeed, to be quite a special way in which conscience is blunted by disobedience and neglect, as we have often been told in solemn warnings from the pulpits; on the other hand, devotion to duty sharpens the edge of conscience itself —a principle which received special emphasis from the Greek philosophers who enjoined their disciples to have particular regard for the judgment of good men. How extensively our power of discerning our duty is affected by our conduct is not easily determined, and there are many matters that would require to be considered if we were to examine that question carefully; we should have to note especially the difference between the failure of judgment that is due to lack of serious attention to the problem—a matter which is in no way peculiar to ethics —and the real distorting of vision in consequence of

[1] *Op. cit.*, p. 43, note A.

44

sin. Moral philosophers have not always made this distinction, and they have encountered some serious trouble in consequence. But we have not to raise these questions here. It will suffice for our purpose to make the admission that, in one way or another, wrongdoing tends to distort our ethical judgments.

So much we readily grant. But we have also to insist that there is much ethical blindness which cannot be ascribed in this way to wrongful choice in the past. This seems especially evident where erroneous ethical judgments are due to ignorance of facts; and the greater part of our moral perplexities and defective ethical beliefs can be traced to this source, as moral philosophers have stressed especially in recent years.[1] It seems particularly foolish to hold that inability to discover the true nature of the situations in which we have to act can invariably be traced to some wickedness on our own part or that of others. Some philosophers have indeed held that view but their adherence to it has only been possible because of fundamental confusions in their thinking. This was the case with T. H. Green who asserted that ill effects could never follow from an honest or conscientious action. Green could only hold this view because of his proneness to discount effects other than the growth of conscientiousness. But it will be very hard for anyone who views this matter clearly to deny that honest and well-meaning persons are sometimes mistaken about the effects of their actions, and that in this way at least they may be mistaken about their duties. Consider a very common case of perplexity—the problem of deciding how to vote at an election. There are many matters to be considered here, and among them questions of an economic character which are particularly difficult to answer and about which

[1] Cf. A. E. Taylor, 'Some Features of Butler's Ethics,' *Mind*, July, 1926.

the experts hold very divided views. Then we have to determine how resolute a particular party will be in attempting to implement its policy, and the kind of parliamentary situation in which it is likely to set about this task. When we have scrutinised a particular policy and considered the relation of what is most desirable to what seems most practicable on the whole, we have yet to form our judgment of personal matters such as the character and suitability of a particular candidate. All this, and a host of other matters enter into the problem how we should cast our vote. And accordingly, while we should not be precluded from holding very strong convictions, there is nothing to warrant the confidence which excludes the possibility of error and ascribes the differing opinions of others to faults of character. Social relationships would become anarchic if differences of opinion amounted to an aspersion on one another's character. Democracy would be speedily ended. Some opinions are indeed more suspect than others, and honest persons should not always be allowed to obey their consciences. But a right ordering of our relations as members of society would be facilitated if we accustomed ourselves to draw a sharper distinction than we do between moral ignorance and moral defects of character, especially in our attitude towards large groups such as a nation or a class. But even if confusion of thought and prejudice distort our judgment of these matters in important regards, no person who attends to the question with any seriousness is likely to deny that there are perplexities, arising from the problematic effects of many of our actions, which are not in any way proportionate to the honesty we bring to the consideration of the course of our duty or the constancy of our devotion to it. With the best will in the world we may be grievously in error. This seems to me to be altogether beyond dispute.

It seems also plain that such errors as arise from a defect in our properly ethical judgment, i.e. from our attempt to appraise the ethical significance of the facts in distinction from ascertaining their nature, are not strictly relative to our moral failures and capable of being ascribed entirely to wrong choice in the past on our own part or on that of others. There is no invariable connection between uprightness of heart and soundness of judgment, even where strictly ethical issues are concerned. The fact that obedience to conscience and cultivation of it has an effect on ethical insight does not prove that ethical insight depends on that factor *alone*. If it did we should expect vaster and more frequent fluctuations in our properly ethical judgments than seem to be warranted by the facts. Moral sense is not so unevenly distributed as the intellectual powers of men or their æsthetic sensibilities. On the other hand, it resembles these latter in so far as the variations which we do observe, do not follow a simple and easily established rule.

Finally, if reference is had to the wickedness of other persons than the agent himself, we must press again the question to what extent particular iniquities in the past can be shown to stand in a special relation to the defects in the moral sensibility of this or that person, and, indeed, to the defect that manifests itself at some particular time. If it be denied that there is such a relation, and held that we must simply ascribe moral blindness to the sinfulness of men generally in the past, then we must reply that in addition to the general vagueness of this position, it is not easily reconciled with the variations, not perhaps as extensive as might appear at first, which we do find in the reliability of the strictly ethical judgments of different persons. Should we not all be affected equally by ethical blindness if this has its source in some accumulated or collective sinfulness of men generally and is not to be connected with some particular wrong acts in the past?

If it be urged that the blindness in question is not to be identified with the ignorance or error of this or that person about the course of his duty in particular circumstances, then the onus of showing what precisely it does mean rests on the theologian. It is not a task to which he brings much enthusiasm.

My contention then is that there is much defective and distorted ethical vision which is not to be ascribed to wickedness or wrongful choice on the part of the individual himself or another. And if the actions we perform in obedience to faulty consciences in these cases are to be accounted sinful, there appears to be sin which does not stand even in an indirect relation to an abuse of moral freedom. This is quite sufficient to ruin the particular attempt of Professor Quick to retain the idea of a sinfulness that pervades human nature and also to ascribe all moral evils to wrong acts of choice on the part of individuals— to come to terms with the fundamental demand of the moral consciousness and hold by the idea of a sinfulness that is inescapable in the life of particular persons.

But that is not all. For even if it could be maintained with some show of plausibility that there is a correlation between deliberate wrongful action and all ethical blindness, or if we were to confine ourselves to the cases where a faulty conscience is in fact the result of neglect or disobedience on the part of the agent himself, yet it would have to be stressed that it is only the wrongful act in the past, and not what we do unavoidably and with good intention to-day, that is sinful. The effects of sin, even within our own nature, are not themselves sins; nor is the heinousness of sin to be estimated in terms of these, or any other effects. Nothing can be put into the reckoning that we do not intend. So much at least seems certain and elementary, however difficult the problem of moral responsibility may be in other regards.

Quick tries to anticipate this objection by drawing a "distinction between sin and guilt."[1] "All acts are sinful in so far as they are wrong and contrary to God's will. But the agent in such an act incurs guilt only in so far as he is blameworthy, because personally responsible, for sinning. And the agent is personally responsible, guilty, and blameworthy for his act, only if he knew, or could at the time have known, it to be wrong and sinful, and could in the light of that knowledge have acted differently."[2] We have to distinguish "(a) between formal and material sin, and (b) between the *reatus* of sin and its *vitium*. Material sin covers every action which considered in itself is wrong and sinful; formal sin is committed only through the wrong choice of an individual who both could and ought to have chosen differently. Again the *reatus* of sin is the sinfulness for which the agent is responsible through his free choice to do wrong when he might have done right; the *vitium* of sin is the evil influence from past sins which renders the individual here and now unable to choose and do right. Thus formal sin alone involves the agent in *reatus* or guilt."[3]

It is not made plain whether there could be any "material sin" without some degree of 'formal sin' on the part of the agent himself. The most that is clear is that "the individual is never solely to blame for his wrong acts."[4] Where "sin is transmitted . . . personal responsibility for acting sinfully is diminished."[5] But "wrong choice for which the individual is responsibile is indeed a real element in sin."[6] If this means that there is always some amount of wilful wrongdoing in sinful acts the position is made to

[1] *Op. cit.*, p. 47.　　[2] *Op. cit.*, p. 47.
[3] *Op. cit.*, p. 47.　　[4] *Op. cit.*, p. 46.
[5] *Op. cit.*, p. 43, note B.　　[6] *Op. cit.*, p. 46.

appear less repugnant to the requirements of the moral consciousness. But there is in fact no warrant for the assumption in question on Quick's premises. 'Material sin' on the part of a particular person need stand in no special relation to formal sin—as we have shown.

But that is not the main matter. The real issue at the moment is whether 'material *sin*' is a proper designation of acts which the agent did not know to be wrong and which "he could not help committing."[1] And I maintain that it is not. We only confuse the issue by retaining the word 'sin' in this reference. For, whatever may be the uses of this word in theological writings in the past, the word can hardly fail to convey to us some impression of genuine wickedness. And even if this were not the case it would still be highly misleading to use the same word for genuine moral evil and for some defect for which the individual is not to be blamed himself. We may indeed quite properly deplore the performance of 'materially' wrong acts, not merely because of their effects, but also because of the condition of mind they reflect. But both these are bad in the sense in which error in general and lack of intellectual discernment or æsthetic sensibility are bad. We are here in the sphere of non-moral as distinct from properly moral value. But sin is essentially a *moral* disvalue, it is a peculiar kind of failure, one in which the person himself is involved in a unique way and to which the ideas of blame and remorse are invariably relevant. As such it must always be wilful.

Quick, I think, manages to make this requirement less embarrassing for himself by the supposition that there is a close concomitance between 'formal' and 'material' sin, the latter, like the former, being ultimately ascribed to a misuse of freedom. For this, as we have seen, there is no foundation. And the contrary assumption that there is,

[1] *Op. cit.*, p. 47.

serves only to show that, in spite of the seemingly genuine admission of the importance of the individual and of freedom of choice, Quick has not seriously related his view to the course of the moral life as we are normally aware of it. He is still thinking of some abstract humanity, of some evil which marks the human situation as a whole and is far removed from the evil-doing of particular persons and the variations in moral value or disvalue which the moral philosopher usually studies.

What little importance Quick really ascribes to the idea of freedom can be seen when we view his doctrine of sin in its relation to other aspects of his theological system as a whole. The ideas of atonement and redemption seem to have significance for him mainly in connection with 'material sin.' He speaks of a 'mighty act of victory' by which Christ, in his death and resurrection, brought expiation and new life. The emphasis is especially upon the power of the 'new life' to break the dominion of sin and release mankind from the 'doom of death' under which it, and indeed the whole of its natural environment, lies. We see how well the notion of a 'fallen nature,' and the burden of a sinfulness which man is unable to cast from himself, fits into this scheme. But it is not plain what part is played in it by deliberate evil choice. If the latter has a part, and is more than an incidental concession to the moral consciousness, it seems at any rate a minor one where the 'eschatology of the new world' is concerned. The great issues seem to turn on the *vitium* of sin rather than the *reatus* for which individual guilt is incurred— the reverse of what we should expect since the latter seems much more fundamental even if the former be allowed, for the moment, to be a form of sin.

It appears, then, that Quick, by his special presentation of traditionalist doctrine, is not providing a really substantial and helpful modification of beliefs in the inevitability of sin, beliefs which are made much more consistent internally by frank repudiation of individual freedom and of the distinction between the 'big sinner' and the 'little sinner.' Before we turn to consider those beliefs more closely I should like to refer to a further feature of Quick's doctrine which illumines the positions we have just considered in some significant ways. It will also bring out in a further way the proneness of the theologian to be at variance with the moral philosopher.

It has already been observed that Professor Quick ascribes every form of evil to an abuse of freedom. Chapter I of his book is mainly concerned with this topic. The author very properly rejects the theories which treat evil as an illusion or a mere 'privation of being.' Evil is positive and altogether real. But "the ultimate source of evil in the world is the free act of the finite and created will which uses its freedom to do wrong and to disobey the will of God."[1]

This theory immediately encounters the difficulty that there seem to be many forms of evil not attributable to human agency. Such are many forms of ignorance, error, bad taste, and suffering. Even when these are due to acts of will there is little likelihood that the evil result is commensurate with the evil intended. The intention may even be good. But Quick replies to this objection by the simple expedient of denying outright that such 'evils' are really evil except in so far as they can be attributed to sinful actions. He refers to "cruelty in sub-human nature,"[2] and notes that the very use of the word cruelty implies moral condemnation. "Our unreflecting use of language is witness to the fact that we regard the problem of evil as fundamentally a moral problem."[3] But this is surely to overstress a verbal point. The fact that stands

[1] *Op. cit.*, p. 31.   [2] *Op. cit.*, p. 27.   [3] *Op. cit.*, p. 28.

out is that there is considerable suffering among animals and children, as well as unmerited suffering and other ills among adult human beings, none of which can reasonably be ascribed to a purposive agency. And it is not true that when these are thought to be 'devoid of any moral significance'[1] "the very problem which they raise begins to disappear."[2] Indeed, as we shall stress, the evils in question present the philosophy of religion with a problem that is all the more acute because they cannot be ascribed to moral agency. Admittedly, a "thumb-screw derives its nature and existence from man's purpose to torture,"[3] but the pain which it causes is evil in itself and a distinct evil from the evil intent to torture. To assert that "pain is not really evil in itself," that "error, in so far as it is positively evil, and not a mere defect in knowledge . . . is the consequence of a wrong act of will,"[4] that the 'germ of the disease' (should we not say the disease itself) is only evil if "we suppose that it has been brought into being . . . by some spiritual will,"[5] seems altogether contrary to the plain truth. This, in fact, is evidenced by the remarkable expedient to which the author has recourse when he refers to the possibility of a 'fallen world soul' or the 'fallen angels' the belief in which may "claim support in Jewish and Christian tradition."[6] A theory that has to summon a *diabolus ex machina* to its support in this fashion shows that it has no foundation other than a doctrinal presumption pushed to the point of theoretical perversity.

[1] *Op. cit.*, p. 28. [2] *Op. cit.*, p. 28. [3] *Op. cit.*, p. 31.
[4] *Op. cit.*, p. 33. [5] *Op. cit.*, p. 32.
[6] *Op. cit.*, p. 29. This belief is however, still very widely held. It is commended, for example, by C. C. J. Webb in his *Problems in the Relation of God and Man*, pp. 267 ff. There is, of course, no inherent objection to the notion of evil spirits other than human beings, but that this should be seriously considered to afford a way of dealing with the problem of evil seems to me very strange.

I do not wish, however, to discuss this matter closely. For the treatment of the problem of evil in general takes us beyond the scope of this essay. But the attitude adopted by Professor Quick here has a bearing on the topics with which we are concerned. For consider how his theory is simplified throughout by the adoption of the view we have noted.

Firstly, there is the point with which, as I remarked, we are not much concerned here—namely, that the problem of evil is considerably simplified if it is held that there is no evil other than moral evil or the result of it. Some difficulties would still remain, and they would be quite acute for certain types of monistic philosophies such as idealism. How is moral evil to be reconciled with the notion of a universe that is perfect throughout or with the belief in an infinitely wise and omnipotent creator? But the problem of moral evil as a problem in theology or the philosophy of religion is very considerably lightened by the fact that the possibility of doing evil is a condition of the attainment of moral worth. There is nothing that seriously disturbs any reasonable belief that we want to hold about the power and goodness of God in the notion of "a divine self-limitation"[1] by which creatures are brought into being capable of moral evil if this has the purpose of making moral good possible. It is the evils not attributable to an "abuse of freedom" that create the most serious difficulty.

Some of these evils can be shown to serve a good purpose that compensates for them or to be among the conditions within which certain values—for example, certain qualities of mind and character—can be realized. But there are certain ills, such as unmerited suffering and especially certain deformities of mind and body and the suffering of children, which do not seem to come under

[1] *Op. cit.*, p. 18.

any of the rational explanations of evil.[1] It is here, at any rate, that religious thinking is put most severely to the test by the spectacle of purposeless evil. It would therefore be a great gain for religious doctrines if, as seems altogether impossible, all evil could be related directly to evil willing.

But that is not the main point for us. For the expedient by which the problem of evil generally is simplified in the way described can also be used to simplify the difficulties that confront us when we turn to consider the only kind of evil that is now allowed to be real—moral evil.

It happens thus. A very extensive part of our duty consists of obligations to produce what is good in a non-moral sense, for example to increase knowledge or happiness and to alleviate suffering. No one can be held responsible for intellectual or cultural shortcomings, and this is why we speak of non-moral values in this reference. But it is a part of our duty to do what we can to produce what is good in this way for ourselves and others. On some views all our duties come under this general utilitarian principle. But there seem to be two ways in which it is possible for us to have further duties. Firstly it may be urged, without departing from the utilitarian view, that we ought to promote the future moral goodness of ourselves and others.[2] In the second place, there may be

[1] This has been very fully exhibited by Professor C. A. Campbell in his paper, 'Reason and the Problem of Suffering,' *Philosophy*, April, 1935.

[2] Whether, in fact, this is to be considered a duty will depend largely on the view we take of the kind of choice in the exercise of which moral freedom consists. If it is held that there must be genuinely open possibilities between which the agent chooses, then it does not seem possible for me now to act in any way which will affect my own moral worth or that of others in the future. For that will depend on my reaction to the alternatives that present themselves at the time; see below, Chapter XI. But the issue is not very important for the present purpose.

duties, such as the duty to tell the truth, which do not depend altogether on a tendency which their performance has to increase the sum of goodness in the world. This is what the intuitionist holds. But if the distinction between moral and non-moral values is blurred, the situation in which it is most apparent that we can be mistaken about the course of our duty is obscured; for the most obvious kind of moral error and perplexity is that which arises directly from our uncertainty about the effectiveness of various courses of action to produce the consequences that have most worth in themselves. If we could remove that kind of perplexity the difficulty that besets the balancing of duties to produce what is good against any further duties we may have would also be considerably modified. It follows that, whether or not we think there are duties besides the duty to produce what is good in the non-moral sense, the inability to appreciate the distinctiveness of non-moral value and to contrast it sharply with the moral worth of the will which directs itself to the ends whose promotion is presumed to be our duty, will carry with it the proneness to regard the content of our duty as standing in some such relation to the quality of the will to perform it as to make ignorance of its nature, if not itself a form of moral wickedness, at least an invariable concomitant. In other words, the failure to distinguish between moral and non-moral values makes it easier to conclude that ethical blindness is itself morally evil or sinful.

It also makes it easier to overlook the peculiar conditions of moral evil and its dependence on the intention of the agent. There is a vague assimilation of moral evil to the evils which do not depend on our will. In consequence, the acknowledgment of the importance of individual choice has to be worked into a general and very vague picture of evil but little related to the actual course of ethical conduct. In this way, as well as in the absurdity of a choice which does not presuppose alternatives with worth and claims of their own, the denial of the independent character of non-moral evil shows us how far removed we are, in the present doctrine of sin, from the specific situations in which men have to act from day to day; the particular choices which we normally take to determine our merit and demerit become absorbed in some universal choice to accept or reject the guidance of God. And here, behind the shallow disguises, we perceive very clearly the same idea of inevitable and universal sin which is presented in a more consistent and unvarnished form by some more uncompromising Protestant theologians. Let us resume our discussion of them.

CHAPTER V

UNIVERSAL SIN

WE HAVE BEEN DISCUSSING the attempt to avoid the severities of a thoroughgoing doctrine of the fall and a corrupt human nature, as instanced in a thinker such as Brunner, by combining in a final theory of sin both the idea of a "marred" human nature and the view of sin as an abuse of freedom of choice. We saw that one of the main difficulties which this view encounters is that of giving a satisfactory account of the relation between the two kinds of sinfulness. But this is only a special mode of the difficulty which arises on any form of the theory of a corrupted human nature, whether as a partial or a complete account of sin, namely that of explaining the relation of the sinfulness in which men generally are steeped to the sinful acts of individual persons and the variation in our estimates of one another's moral worth.

If sinfulness could be thought of on the analogy of a disease the problem would be very much simplified. The members of a family may be tainted with a disease that is hereditary in that family without succumbing in the same measure to that disease. But this is just the analogy we cannot apply. Sin implies guilt and responsibility, and we cannot retain these ideas, in any properly ethical sense, if we assimilate moral evil to ill-health. This is implied in the refusal of the theologians who emphasize most the universality of sin to identify this universality with abstract similarity or mere causal connection. What they have in mind is more the implication of one person in the sin of another, or some pervasive guilt by which our actions as a whole are affected. The sin of Adam is the sin of each, there is a literal sameness about

58

its universality. And it is just because it obscures the issue in this critical regard that the metaphor of an evil taint is most misleading.

The real issue then is whether or not it is meaningful to speak of a sinfulness of 'man.' It is at this point that the moral philosopher finds himself most mystified by the theologian, for however much the former may be overwhelmed by the problem of freedom and responsibility, his work is not complicated by the idea of a sinfulness that does not vary from one individual to another. It is a variable quality that he studies and he will be very suspicious, for that reason, of pronouncements about the moral character of 'man,' of 'humanity' and the 'race.' To speak of the sinfulness of 'man' obscures, and if taken strictly contradicts, that very variability of moral worth which the moral philosopher tries to describe.

Some theologians take a bold course in this matter. And the tribute must be paid them of avoiding much prevarication. They openly repudiate the idea that there is a 'big sinner' and a 'little sinner.' 'All men have sinned,' and while the results and manifestations of this universal sinfulness vary, the essential evil remains the same in every action and in the life of every person. This essential evil is normally regarded as a pride or selfishness by which personality as a whole is affected. The effort to avoid evil is itself a form of sinful self-assertion. Indeed there are writers who are not averse from regarding the attempt of man to overcome his sinful nature as the supreme manifestation of his perverted nature. The more he struggles the more he is caught in the meshes of his sin.

Now if it were merely asserted that all human actions are, in fact, selfish, the position would be quite consistent and intelligible. It is a position that has been ingeniously defended by several thinkers. But the corollary of that position is, clearly, that man is neither moral nor immoral, that moral responsibility in the proper sense is an illusion

But if it be held, in defiance of normal belief, that guilt can be incurred by a propensity which we cannot escape, it does seem much the more reasonable course to regard all as equally guilty. This is the view of the strict traditionalist. But to preclude comparisons between the moral worth of particular persons in this way seems to do complete violence to what we feel normally bound to think.

It is not contended that comparisons of this kind are easy. On the contrary, it must be admitted that they are extremely difficult, and no one should presume to make strictures on the moral worth of another individual without the utmost caution. Normally such strictures are to be avoided, for there is so much that requires to be known before any final judgment is passed, and so much that is bound to be hidden from public view, that the likelihood of arriving at a sound conclusion is highly problematic. Condemnation of outward conduct is of course another matter, although there is ample room for humility and caution here as well. But overt action, even when it can be presumed that the intention corresponds to the actual result, is a most incomplete indication of the moral quality of the person. This we can confidently state without committing ourselves to any final account of the criteria of moral value. The assurance with which moral strictures are sometimes made by certain individuals upon others is evidence of a nauseating inability to understand the complications of human character and the moral life, and it is this stupidity in particular that the theologians we have been discussing are most prone to instance as evidence of the sinful nature of man— albeit that is not the true explanation of the facts. But we are none the less bound to make estimates of one another's moral worth, and there seem also to be situations which warrant the expression of the opinions we form, not only about the 'material' or outward rightness of conduct but also about the inner and properly moral quality of the life which they reveal. And even if it had to be admitted that the uncertainty which attends the latter kind of judgment in particular were such as to preclude any judgment other than the condemnation or approval of outward conduct, this would in no whit affect the fact that there are extensive differences in moral quality between one kind of conduct and another. The difficulty of ascertaining the facts and ascribing to the facts that we can discover their proper importance, a difficulty which is by no means absent from the appraisal of the worth of even our own conduct, does not in any way affect the finality of the distinctions of value which do qualify those facts. This presumption is essential to any ethical attitude.

To assert that all men are 'equally sinful' seems therefore a complete repudiation of the presumption upon which ordinary ethical thinking proceeds. It is an 'interpretation' which, as Professor Tennant observes, "would seem to make an end at once of ethics and Christian theology."[1] But such in point of fact is the position adopted by some extremely influential theologians at the present time.

One of these is Reinhold Niebuhr. Niebuhr is not unaware of the peculiarly difficult and paradoxical nature of his view. But the device to which he is reduced in the attempt to overcome obvious objections serves to make it plainer how much the position depends on confusion of thought.

Niebuhr admits that the doctrine of the 'equality of sin' "imperils and seems to weaken all moral judgments which deal with the 'nicely calculated less and more' of justice and goodness as revealed in the relativities of

---

[1] *The Concept of Sin*, p. 265.

history."[1] Accordingly, while he insists as emphatically as Barth "that these distinctions should disappear at the ultimate religious level of judgment,"[2] he warns us also against "the tendency of orthodox Protestantism to efface all moral distinctions of history in the light of a religious conviction of the undifferentiated sinfulness of all men."[3] We must continue to respect the "relative moral achievements of history,"[4] but this must somehow be achieved without prejudice to "the proposition that all men are equally sinners in the sight of God."[5] How is this possible?

The answer turns on a curious distinction between sin and guilt. "All men are sinners," but "there is nevertheless an ascertainable inequality of guilt among men in the actualities of history. Guilt is distinguished from sin in that it represents the objective and historical consequences of sin, for which the sinner must be held responsible."[6] "Guilt is the objective consequence of sin," and "it is important to recognize that Biblical religion has emphasized this inequality of guilt just as much as the equality of sin."[7] "Men who are equally sinners in the sight of God need not be equally guilty of a specific act of wrongdoing in which they are involved."[8] It is to the 'guilt' of men that the 'less and more' of 'historical moral judgments' refers.

What merit has this suggestion? Very little, I fear.

Objection may be taken, in the first place, to the misuse of the word 'guilt.'[9] In the normal and accepted usage this word refers to a quality of the will of the agent and not

---

[1] *The Nature and Destiny of Man*, p. 233. [2] *Op. cit.*, p. 234.
[3] *Op. cit.*, p. 235. [4] *Op. cit.*, p. 234.
[5] *Op. cit.*, p. 233. [6] *Op. cit.*, p. 235.
[7] *Op. cit.*, p. 236. [8] *Op. cit.*, p. 236.
[9] The use, incidentally, is diametrically opposed to that of Quick. See above, p. 49.

to the objective consequences of action. This is a terminological objection and there would be no need to press it very closely, since terms have often to be adapted to a special purpose in a technical reference, were it not for the cover it affords to serious confusion of thought.

Niebuhr really proceeds on the entirely misleading assumption that there are no variations of ethical judgment to be considered besides variations in the outward 'more and less' of justice that we produce. But there is also in fact a variation in the properly moral value of the person that is not strictly proportionate to the course of events which his action initiates. This we have already stressed. And if the point be allowed, as it seems to me it must unless we are to give up the attempt to understand the moral life, then we are committed to the admission that there is a variation in 'sinfulness' if the term is to be used in anything approximating its ordinary usage. It is this that is obscured by the ambiguous use of the words 'guilt' and 'responsibility' to designate the outward injustices we perpetrate. For the normal associations of the words with final moral distinctions suggest that we have explained all that requires to be explained when we have made an admission of variations in the actual effects of action.

There appears, in fact, to be no point of contact between the doctrine of the 'equality of sin' and any recognisable ethical thinking. But can we empty the consciousness of sin in this way of all ethical import? Does the word 'sin' stand for something altogether different from the immorality of this or that person, the evil-doing which we condemn in others and for which we feel the pangs of remorse in our own case? If that is so let our procedure be clear. Let it be allowed that we are coining a new language, and let us make an end of bewildering the ordinary reader by pretending to be discussing what has normally been understood by such terms as 'guilt' and 'sin.'

The unwillingness of Niebuhr himself to take such a step and to regard himself as describing some aspect of religious life altogether different from the moral one is evidenced in the special appeal that he himself makes to the feelings of 'remorse or repentance' in support of his claim that men remain responsible in spite of the 'inevitability of sin.'[1] The result of this attitude is *to divorce the consciousness of sin and the 'uneasy conscience' altogether from the business of living*—a divorce that cannot fail to have a serious effect upon practice as well as on religious thinking. This is fully borne out when we consider how this 'equal sinfulness' of men is conceived.

Niebuhr does not think that man is a sinner by nature. His nature was given him by God who cannot be the author of evil. But the nature of man is such as to expose him to temptation. This is because man is finite and also aware of the limitations of a finite mind. "He stands at the juncture of nature and spirit"[2] and thus "being both free and bound, both limited and limitless, is anxious. . . . Anxiety is the internal description of the state of temptation. . . . Yet anxiety is not sin. It must be distinguished from sin partly because it is its precondition and not its actuality and partly because it is the basis of all human creativity as well as the precondition of sin."[3] "The basic source of temptation resides . . . in the inclination of man either to deny the contingent character of his existence (in pride and self-love) or to escape from his freedom [in sensuality]"[4]—"unlimited devotion to limited values." Anxiety thus "brings forth pride and sensuality,"[5] but it is not inevitable from the 'human situation' itself that man should seek this solution to the "contradiction of

[1] *Op. cit.*, pp. 270-6.   [2] *Op. cit.*, p. 193.
[3] *Op. cit.*, p. 195.   [4] *Op. cit.*, p. 197.
[5] *Op. cit.*, p. 198.

finiteness and freedom."[1] For God, on the Christian view, "is revealed as loving will; and His will is active in creation, judgment, and redemption. The highest self-realization for the self is therefore not the destruction of its particularity, but the subjection of its particular will to the universal will."[2] But this is not in fact achieved because "the self lacks the faith and trust to subject itself to God. It seeks to establish itself independently. It seeks to find its life and thereby loses it."[3] "The sin of inordinate self-love thus points to the prior sin of lack of trust in God."[4] "The anxiety of freedom leads to sin only if the prior sin of unbelief is assumed."[5] "Sin posits itself." What, then, causes the sin of unbelief? The answer here is that evil enters the "situation of finiteness and freedom . . . prior to any human action." This is "expressed in Biblical thought by the conception of the devil. The devil is a fallen angel, who fell because he sought to lift himself above his measure and who in turn insinuates temptation into human life. The sin of each individual is preceded by Adam's sin: but even this first sin of history is not the first sin. One may, in other words, go further back than human history and still not escape the paradoxical conclusion that the situation of finiteness and freedom would not lead to sin if sin were not already introduced into the situation."[6] A 'false interpretation' is placed by man upon his own situation at the suggestion of "a force of evil which precedes his own sin,"[7] "a principle or force of evil antecedent to any evil human action. Before man fell the devil fell."[8] And man is involved in his 'fall.'

Man's freedom does not thus consist in a power to choose to do good or ill. It must rather be understood as

<hr />

[1] *Op. cit.*, p. 190.   [2] *Op. cit.*, p. 267.   [3] *Op. cit.*, p. 267.
[4] *Op. cit.*, p. 268.   [5] *Op. cit.*, p. 268.   [6] *Op. cit.*, p. 270.
[7] *Op. cit.*, p. 193.   [8] *Op. cit.*, p. 192.

the way "man as spirit transcends the temporal and natural process in which he is involved and also transcends himself."[1] He stands "under seemingly[2] limitless possibilities"[3] and "he can do nothing and regard it perfectly done, because higher possibilities are revealed in each achievement."[4] It is in the attempt to overcome the contingent character of his existence, not by subjecting himself to God, but by self assertion or 'self-deification',[5] that man falls into the sin of pride; and sensuality, as we have seen, is man's attempt to escape from "his unlimited possibilities of freedom."[6] In his sinfulness man thus finds the proof of his freedom, and he "is most free in the discovery that he is not free."[7] "Human freedom is most perfectly discovered and asserted in the realization of the bondage of the will."[8] As the paradox is also phrased: "The ultimate proof of the freedom of the human spirit is its own recognition that its will is not free to choose between good and evil."[9] "It is within and by his freedom that man sins. The final paradox is that the discovery of the inevitability of sin is man's highest assertion of freedom."[10] We must not sacrifice this paradox to "a premature logical consistency."[11]

[1] *Op. cit.*, p. 266.

[2] It is not altogether clear how far Niebuhr wishes to maintain that man can be said to be unlimited in so far as he transcends his limitations by knowing them. "Man's knowledge is limited by time and place. Yet it is not as limited as animal knowledge. The proof that it is not so limited is given by the fact that man knows something of these limits, which means that in some sense he transcends them" (p. 194). But we are also warned that "there are, of course, limits, but it is difficult to gauge them from any immediate perspective. There is therefore no limit of achievement in any sphere of activity in which human history can rest with equanimity" (p. 196). We also hear of man's "unlimited and his limited knowledge" (p. 193). He is "limited and limitless" (p. 194).

[3] *Op. cit.*, p. 196. [4] *Op. cit.*, p. 196. [5] *Op. cit.*, p. 213.
[6] *Op. cit.*, p. 198. [7] *Op. cit.*, p. 276. [8] *Op. cit.*, p. 276.
[9] *Op. cit.*, p. 274. [10] *Op. cit.*, p, 279. [11] *Op. cit.*, p. 279.

Niebuhr tries to bring this view more into accord with ordinary thought by protesting, in the words of Kierkegaard and with a belated ardour[1] that cannot fail to be suspect, that " 'The concept of sin and guilt presupposes the individual as individual. There is no concern for his relation to any cosmic or past totality. The only concern is that he is guilty.' "[2] But the quotation continues: " 'and yet he is supposed to become guilty through fate, the very fate about which there is no concern. And thereby he becomes something which resolves the concept of fate, and to become that through fate. If this contradiction is wrongly understood it leads to false concepts of original sin. Rightly understood it leads to a true concept, to the idea namely that every individual is itself and the race, and that the later individual is not significantly differentiated from the first man.' "[3]

These views seem to be altogether untenable as they stand. I do indeed also think that they have much importance. To that I shall return. It must also be admitted that, while there is a great deal of obscurantism and much slurring over elementary distinctions, as exemplified above,[4] in a way that almost invites an accusation of theological blustering, there is also much forthrightness and a skilfulness in the presentation of a difficult view; there is a discerning scholarship and shrewd psychological insight. But none of this avails to build up a reasonable doctrine. For the picture as a whole is thrown entirely out of focus by a failure to distinguish between ethical and religious truth and to relate the former effectively to the religious life as a whole.

[1] In the last passage of the chapter on 'Sin and Man's Responsibility,' which, following the two long chapters on 'Man as Sinner,' concludes the main discussion of this topic.

[2] *Op. cit.*, p. 279.   [3] *Op. cit.*, p. 279.   [4] pp. 62, 63.

It is that failure that concerns us here. And I do not think we require anything beyond the brief outline just given to show how remote from life and experience the notion of sin becomes when its properly ethical meaning is dissolved into religious conceptions. In some ways that procedure may simplify the exposition of Scripture, but I feel assured that it does not get at the real meaning even of the passages which seem to lend it most support, much less at the final message of the Scriptures as a whole and the testimony of other notable religious writings. A sinfulness which is as much that of the race as of the individual, which depends on a freedom quite different from the power to choose between good and ill, which is 'introduced into the human situation' and made inevitable by a 'force of evil prior to any human action,' is devoid of relevance to the conduct of individual lives; and for that reason alone it must stand discredited at the bar of ethics.

It will not improve matters here for the theologian to abuse the 'moralistic' attitude as it is sometimes contemptuously labelled. For ethics is not based upon arbitrary assumptions. It is not just some point of view which we may or may not adopt; it claims to describe what we are bound to believe about the life of man in one most important regard.

The upshot of Niebuhr's doctrine is the presentation of sin, as many are only too prone to regard it to-day, as some mysterious cosmic disaster, some vague blot upon the universe which we just cannot conjure away, something also on account of which we must all bow our heads in shame, and, in particular, something towards which we should adopt certain religious attitudes and about which theological doctrines have to be formed. The preacher must stand in his pulpit at appointed times to pronounce himself 'agin it,' and to announce the way of salvation. But none of this appears to touch the individual in the conduct of his life, and however much he may be induced to give formal assent to his own involvement in the sins of the world, he remains fundamentally serene in the assurance that it does not really concern him for the simple reason that there was nothing he could have done about it.

The Protestant Reformation was not in fact Protestant enough; for it conveyed its protest against the authoritarianism of the mediæval Church too much within the assumptions about the individual upon which that Church proceeded and to which the abuses which the Reformers found most offensive were very directly due. In this way, while seeming to provide a remedy, and actually succeeding in large measure to cure the immediate and grosser manifestations of a great evil, it in fact lent a new and long lease of life to a view that strikes at the heart of true religion. That view, to put it bluntly, is the view that religion can be managed by proxy. This was never completely and overtly the teaching of the mediæval Church, and it could not be so any more than the practices it prompted could be altogether vicious, when the repository in which the individual was to place his religious life was a visible institution whose pretensions could never be so overwhelming as to belie its real character altogether. In some ways indeed the individual had much better standing in the teaching of the Roman Church than in the theology and practice of the Reformers. It was Luther who announced that "Free-will lies prostrate"; and high and substantial privileges which the individual has come to enjoy with the development of a democratic way of life, to which Protestantism made such an important contribution, are also seriously imperilled, especially in the growing complexities of modern life, by lack of some of those very safeguards which protected him from complete exploitation in mediæval times. This is a familiar story by now, and we can hardly add anything to the telling of it here; neither is it to the purpose to balance at all closely the indebtedness in practice of the individual to one movement or the other. There have been concessions on both sides, and practice has not always conformed to principle; moreover many threads besides explicitly ethical and religious ones have gone to the weaving of European civilization as we know it. But I think, nonetheless, that we can trace very clearly the influence of the perpetuation in Western religious thought of a view which could not properly accommodate the individual; and however considerable the benefits that accrued initially through the modification of the earlier form of that view, the form in which it has been perpetuated may spell grimmer disasters to-day than those to be accounted to it in the past. For an intangible cosmology has now to fill the role once ascribed to the church as the vicarious bearer and trustee of the individual's religious interests. This isolates religion much more completely from life; it leaves the individual impotent and insignificant while the great cosmic forces run their play through to its appointed end. He is more a cipher than he could ever be if he left his soul in the keeping of an institution.

It need hardly be stressed how much the crisis of Western civilization turns on a true estimate of the individual; neither need we detail here the factors that conspire to eclipse him or consider what adjustment of modern conditions will make for the truest development of persons. These are problems that will tax our energies to the utmost. But it will also be evident without elaboration how impossible of solution those problems will be, and how swiftly disaster will follow, if the very springs of individual responsibility are dried up in an apathetic surrender to oppressive doctrinal fictions.

There is no need of measured terms here. For if the analysis I have given is correct the situation is a really grave one. It has to be remembered that the volume by Reinhold Niebuhr to which I have referred is the first of two series of Gifford Lectures. It is intended to command the most serious attention. And the fact that it is possible to fly in the face of elementary ethical principles and present us, in a work meant to carry its influence far, with a view which can only compensate for a complete repudiation of the moral life by an attenuated lip service, is, I think, no slight indication of the quality and trend of our thinking in the present crisis of civilization. Never was there more urgent need to raise the level of thought to that of other creative energies, and to infuse into ordinary living a consciousness of ethical realities proof against the enervating influences of mechanization and the confusions of an age of transition. If we cease to have a serious regard for morality, if the ideas of obligation and accountability become crusted over, the result will be a sickening of other creative energies. Art will become dilettante and its vitality will be sapped. There will be no stark moral reality to give it body, and this will lead to substitutes and palliatives that will only serve to drain all the more rapidly the energies they can neither produce nor nourish. In vain shall we try to cut our losses and make the best we can of a cultural civilization devoid of true moral consciousness. If ethics goes culture fails also. And in such conditions, wretched enough surely in themselves and charged with all manner of evil possibilities, religion can hardly take root. There can be no true religion without morality.

On these matters there is no need to expatiate. The note of urgency in contemporary theology is indeed rightly sounded, although the solution is so wide of the truth.

This essay is not addressed to those who cannot see that the moral life has to be saved. Its purpose is to show that the prevailing trend in theology to-day is as serious a menace as any to a living morality.

This is not a matter we can pursue in detail. But I should like to refer to a passage where the cynicism that underlies the contempt of the individual in theology to-day shows its really deeprooted and insidious character. It appears in a volume particularly well-known to teachers of theology and one which, incidentally, illustrates extremely well the working out of the assumptions of Protestant thinking to which I have referred. In his *Christian Doctrine*, the Rev. J. S. Whale, after warning his reader of the danger of "exposing yourself to the charge of theological illiteracy," comments in the following terms on the "truth which the doctrine of the Trinity is meant to conserve."[1]

"One might as well tell a mathematician that the square root of minus one is mythological nonsense. He would only raise his eyebrows and ask for your mathematical credentials. The most elementary study of the history and meaning of Christian doctrine suffices to show that though no one 'understands' the vast mystery of the triune God, the doctrine of the Trinity is not unintelligible; it is fundamental to Christian soteriology and as such it demands my serious study if I am to evaluate it critically. If a mathematician found me waxing morally indignant over $A° = 1$ he would soon discover by cross-examination that I was not only criticizing something which I did not understand, but also caricaturing it. Similarly, the doctrine of the Trinity is easily caricatured, but the truths which it presupposes being inescapable, the doctrine itself is in some form inescapable, and anyone who dismisses it with impatience or contempt

[1] *Op. cit.*, p. 95.

will be displaying intellectual sloth rather than intellectual acumen; moreover, he will thereby be evading the very soteriological problems which his criticisms presuppose."[1]

Whale seeks to safeguard himself by remarking also that "Theological formulations are never sacrosanct ... plain men are not necessarily interested in theology. They know that religion is never the preserve of specialists."[2] If "certain elements in the technical language of theology" prove a 'stumbling block,' "their use should be abandoned."[3] "No man is preaching the Gospel who is not expounding its true, historic meaning and 'getting it across.' "[4]

But the mischief is done. The comparison with mathematics is strikingly indicative of a deep estrangement of religion from ordinary thought and experience. Admittedly there is ample room for expert thinking about religious questions, and the character of this thinking will not be readily intelligible to the layman any more than philosophical conclusions or scientific theories will conform directly to 'vulgar' or 'common-sense' notions. But thought has its part in religion at all levels. And the fundamental truths of religion must be capable of apprehension in their main essentials by a person who leads a normal religious life if they are to prove the means of that Christian 'salvation' which operates through the assent or surrender of the 'whole' person. To make the assent irrational and a blind submission to authority belies the 'universal' character of Christianity, the simplicity by which 'weak things and things that are despised' are 'called'; it is a reversal to the mystery-mongering, the cults and priesthoods, of primitive religion. And this, it seems to me, is precisely what is involved in the presentation of notions which ordinary conviction

[1] *Op. cit.*, p. 96. [2] *Op. cit.*, p. 96.
[3] *Op. cit.*, p. 96. [4] *Op. cit.*, p. 96.

must reject outright under the cover of a distinctive religious way of thinking entitled to thrust aside normal assumptions. A large place must be left for revelation in religion. And revelation cannot be rationalized—a matter to which we shall return. But it certainly does not follow that our thought about religion and the thinking that enters into the religious life itself can do any violence it pleases to normal convictions. A final view must have room for these as it must also have place for revelation. And a contempt for that which we feel normally bound to believe is an indication of that wrapping up of religion in doctrinal mysteries and remote systems to which the comparison with mathematics,[1] the study of the expert *par excellence*, affords the most significant insight. Nowhere could the betrayal of Protestantism by itself be more pointedly exhibited than in the use of such an analogy by a leading Protestant teacher.

It is not surprising that Dr. Whale should acquiesce so readily in the notion of a 'sinful mass' and insist that sin has a "solidary aspect"[2] which makes it "never a man's private affair."[3] It is not strange that he should summon to his aid the teaching of recent psychology about the 'collective unconsciousness' and 'inborn forces' whose 'content is not individual but universal, and as such, "beyond the conscious control of the will."[4] We do not

[1] The mathematician, priding himself quite properly on his clarity and consistency, might well resent the comparison on other grounds.

[2] *Op. cit.*, p. 46.   [3] *Op. cit.*, p. 46.

[4] *Op. cit.*, p. 46. There is a marked proneness among theologians to-day to refer to the views of the psychoanalysts in support of their doctrines. But have they forgotten just what the analyst usually thinks about religion and morals? Are they quite clear what sort of an ally they have brought into their camp? If not, let them look again at Freud's *Future of an Illusion* or consider the presentation of Freudian principles in their bearing on morals and religion by J.C. Flugel in his recent *Man, Morals and Society*.

74

marvel that he flies in the face of elementary moral principles in the quotation from Schleiermacher that sin "is in each the work of all: in all the work of each."[1]

[1]*Op. cit.*, p. 46.

CHAPTER VI

COLLECTIVE RESPONSIBILITY

IN OPPOSING TO THE notion of a 'collective' responsibility the belief that responsibility is essentially individual we have, in the final analysis, to appeal to immediate ethical insight. It does seem to me beyond the range of reasonable controversy that no man can answer for another's sin or be guilty of it. But if the matter is disputed, then I know of no argument by which the issue can be settled. I can only insist that the matter seems to me to be very plainly as I have described it and that I find it very hard to understand what can be passing in the minds of those who maintain the contrary with a clear understanding of what they maintain. But the situation allows of some easement. For disputes about ultimate problems prove very often to be due to misconceptions and the absence of a clear analysis; it is through such confusions that bias and prejudice affect our convictions for the most part. Along with the injunction to reflect again we can thus, without claiming that anything can be said to *prove* our position, attempt to remove some common confusions which hinder the free operation of the moral consciousness in regard to this crucial question of 'shared' responsibility.

Advocates of the view that one person enters into the life of another to the extent of participating in his guilt are rather prone to belittle their critics by calling them individualists, and confusions arising from the misuse of this highly ambiguous term have been a source of much fruitless controversy in theology as in other disciplines. Individualism is a term that has been applied to positions that are widely different in important regards—a matter that should induce a great deal of caution in the use of it. But in its main usage the meaning of the term can be clearly indicated. It stands for a predominant feature of social and political thinking in the West in recent centuries. This is the failure to appreciate the nature and extent of the individual's dependence on society and the consequent need to adjust the rights and duties of one person to those of another. Rights and duties are never, in fact, inalienable or absolute; they have to be viewed in their relation to one another within a system of what is right on the whole, the adjustment of particular duties to the general duty of conforming to social procedure being normally paramount. The circumstances of the present time make this very plain, although there are many quarters in which it is not fairly acknowledged. But a zeal for liberty engendered in the fifteenth and sixteenth centuries, turning as was natural in the first instance, to the negative tasks of removing hindrances and oppressive barriers, bequeathed to subsequent centuries a profound suspicion of any interference with the individual which persisted even in those theories, such as idealism, which seem at first sight to be taking fair account of man's dependence on society. This has delayed the progress of important reforms, and we have need to be especially cautioned against this misconception of freedom—all the more insidious because of undoubted benefits for which it proved the vehicle—at a time when failure to give a positive turn to democratic enactment may well be disastrous. Individualism is thus particularly out of accord with the needs of our time, it is a shallow and negative view. But the view which does in this way invite severe censure has no particular bearing on the contention that moral responsibility belongs to the individual and not to society. There is nothing 'atomic' about this latter view in any sense which is reprehensible.

But when it is designated by the term individualism the normal meaning and associations of the term hinder an unprejudiced estimate of the truth of the theory. One is sometimes even tempted to suspect a deliberate exploitation of an unsavoury term.

Closely related to this verbal confusion is the failure to distinguish between responsibility for others and responsibility towards them. Indeed, 'responsibility for' is itself an ambiguous phrase, and is often used in the sense of responsibility 'towards.' An officer may thus be said to be responsible for his platoon in the sense that it rests with him directly, or in the main, to ensure that the needs and requirements of its members are supplied. It is his duty, for example, to provide proper billets for them. A teacher is, in the same way, responsible for his class. In this usage everyone has responsibilities that enter far into the lives of others. We have a certain care which we should show for the interest of others and this is not different in essentials from the more complete responsibility of an official of some kind for a group of persons. All that is really meant is that we have duties towards others, and since most, if not all,[1] of our duties are of this kind, it would be absurd to advance an ethical theory which repudiated 'responsibility for' others in the present sense. At the present time we require to deepen the consciousness of the extensive range of such 'responsibilities.' And if the denial of collective responsibility implied the repudiation of mutual responsibility in the sense of mutual duties, it would be so complete an abrogation of moral ideas, and such a foolish misconception of the dignity of the individual, as to merit all the abuse which has been showered in some quarters upon the notion of individual responsibility. But there is in fact nothing whatsoever in

[1] The question whether it is proper to speak of duties to ourselves has been much debated in recent ethics.

this latter notion to warrant the suggestion that a person need consider no other interest than his own. The point needs to be said all the more emphatically because the elementary character of the confusion charges it with graver possibilities of mischief.

A somewhat complicated form of this confusion is the following. The officer and the teacher, to continue our illustrations, may also be said to be responsible for the groups in their charge, not merely in the sense of having to ensure their welfare, but also in the sense of being answerable for their behaviour. The schoolmaster may have to answer for the mischief perpetrated by his pupil. But this, in the normal and most important sense, is because an important part of the teacher's duties towards his pupils, and towards the community generally, is to train the former in right ways of behaviour and use his influence with them to restrain unruly tendencies. The officer is answerable for the conduct of his troops in the same way—namely, that it is his duty to see that they do conduct themselves in the proper manner; and this is allowed to be his duty only on the presumption that certain conduct on his part, by way of example as well as precept and instruction, will have the desired effect on the conduct of his men. He has the responsibility for acting in certain ways whose justification is exhibited in its effect on the actions of others. But his responsibility ends with that which he has done or neglected to do. It is only in an elliptical sense that one man can be said to be responsible for the conduct of others.

This matter we must pursue a little further. But let us first remove out of the way a subsidiary confusion which is apt to complicate the issue. The parent or teacher or officer may also be said to be responsible for others, not in the properly ethical sense that they have duties to promote the welfare of others or to seek to modify their conduct in certain ways, but merely in the sense that they will be proceeded against if they fail to ensure the results desired. This is the *legal* meaning of responsibility, but it has application to social enactment generally—although it is best exemplified in the enforcement of 'positive' law. It is found convenient for certain practical ends to regard one person as accountable for matters which it is not certain that he could control. The law cannot be scrupulously fair. The risk of minor injustices has to be run in the interest of completer justice on the whole. For this reason a parent is held responsible, within certain limits, not merely for the welfare, but also for the conduct of his children even where it is not assured that any act of his could have modified it. Similarly expediency may require the punishment of an officer for the misconduct of his troops in a way not proportionate to his own negligence or failure. The more discipline can be maintained without such measures the better, but they cannot always be avoided. Another example of vicarious legal responsibility and one that has a very close bearing on the notion of a collective responsibility, is the responsibility in law of a trading company or some similar body. For certain legal purposes, civil and criminal, it is necessary to treat corporations on the same basis as individuals. And just as a parent may have to pay damages or a fine on behalf of his children, so the members of a company may incur liabilities through the misdemeanour of representatives or servants or because of some failure or wrong not traceable to a particular individual. It does not concern us here to enquire with any care what the conditions are which warrant legal procedure against a body of persons jointly. Suffice it to note that the practice, involving much injustice in some regards and, in some cases, legal proceedings against persons presumed to be altogether morally innocent, is the best way of ensuring the greatest justice on the whole in some matters. But legal responsibility is one thing, moral responsibility is another. This does not mean a complete divorce of law from morality, as some critics rather hastily conclude. The law is moral in the sense that the justification for enforcing it lies in the moral ends[1] it serves. But law can only deal directly with outward conduct, and legal guilt, while normally involving some moral guilt, bears no strict or invariable relation to the latter. Legal guilt implies no more than the actual infringement of positive law, and is not in itself an indication of moral value or disvalue; legal and quasi-legal responsibility means only liability to be punished. It is possible to incur this jointly or vicariously. But the meaning of ethical guilt and ethical responsibility is quite different. In a properly ethical reference responsibility means simply the fact that we have duties—in other words it is ultimate and unanalysable; duty or obligation is an ultimate ethical notion. And the fact that there is joint responsibility in law is thus no evidence for joint responsibility in the properly ethical sense. We have thus to be very careful not to confuse the two conceptions.

The failure to distinguish between the legal and the moral meaning of responsibility has been a prime source of confusion in the treatment of the problem of moral freedom generally. But it is in connection with the problem of collective responsibility that it impinges on our problem. For the theological notion of guilt does not in other ways

---

[1] This includes more than the promotion of moral worth in the strict sense. Some political writers and economists, of whom Marshall is a fine example, have committed themselves to a very limited view of State enactment by concentrating on the promotion of conscientious characters, to the neglect of intellectual, æsthetic, and material goods.

follow the legalistic ideas to the same extent as some mistaken ethical doctrines.[1]

Let us return now to the question of one man's 'implication' in the conduct of another. One person may be responsible for the conduct of his fellow in the sense that he has a duty to promote it, not merely in the legal but also in the moral sense of duty. Does it not follow then, it may be urged, that the quality of the conduct to which my action is expected to contribute can be laid in part at my door? Our actions, in other words, influence the actions of others as well as their general well-being. Do we not therefore act jointly in the sense required for collective moral responsibility? I do not think so. For here also my responsibility in the proper moral sense terminates strictly with my part in a joint undertaking. It may not be possible for an outsider to assign his due share of responsibility to each party. But my responsibility in fact ends with what I have done or neglected to do. Consider the case of the man who is tempted by his friend to embezzle the funds of his employer. It might be thought in a case of this kind that the friend was implicated morally in the guilt of the actual criminal. The crime would not have been committed had not the friend held out certain inducements. But the proper account of the matter is that the inducement or encouragement given to the criminal by another does lessen the moral guilt of the criminal, as it would usually lessen his legal guilt, but that he remains solely guilty for the way he has responded to the situation as a whole, including such approaches as his friend or accomplice made to him. The friend

[1] The definition of responsibility as 'liability to punishment'—its legal, but not its moral meaning—has often prepared the way for views of responsibility which do not require final freedom of choice. For two very different examples see F. H. Bradley, *Ethical Studies*, Chapter I, and Hastings Rashdall, *Theory of Good and Evil*, Vol. II, Chapter III, especially p. 334.

would also be guilty, but guilty for his own action in setting certain temptations before another and proceeding in a way which was calculated to turn him from the path of duty. There are two actions and two agents, and each agent bears his own responsibility and guilt; the responsibility cannot be spread out over the undertaking as a whole.

It is worth noting here that when the law does take account of extenuating circumstances it is mainly because less punishment is needed to deter the criminal (or others) from the repetition of a crime committed under special provocation. Moral guilt cannot be estimated with any precision for the purpose of a court of law. But the willingness to allow extenuating circumstances does seem also to some extent an indication of the general recognition that guilt is proportionate to deliberate intention.

Consider again the case instanced by Gomperz of a person who steals under stress of great privation and need. "Are we," he asks, "as indignant as people may have been some hundred years ago when we hear that a poor woman has stolen a loaf of bread to give to her children, or that the son of a drunkard has committed an act of violence? Or, to speak more precisely, is our indignation directed as exclusively against that woman or that man and not, at least in part, rather against a state of things in which children are left without bread and drunkards are free to multiply at their pleasure? . . . Is not society . . . as guilty as he is? And does it not look, therefore, as if responsibility . . . was now being placed, to a considerable extent upon social conditions, structures, and institutions?"[1]

Now it seems clearly true that the guilt of the 'poor woman' or the 'son of a drunkard' is substantially

[1] 'Individual, Social and Collective Responsibility,' *International Journal of Ethics*, Vol. XLIX, p. 329.

mitigated by environmental conditions of the kind indicated. In extreme cases blame would be out of place
altogether. But this does not mean that the blame has to
be transferred to other shoulders. It is possible that no
one is to blame. For trying and provocative circumstances,
even when they spring from social maladjustment,
cannot always be traced to deliberate human agency.
But even if the blame for the circumstances which
conduce to violence and crime can be laid fairly at the
door of particular members of society, it is for their
part in bringing about or maintaining such conditions,
and not for the wrongful actions of the victims of their
neglect or malevolence that they are guilty. If the victim
is also thought to be guilty it is on the presumption that
he could have resisted the temptations to which he was
exposed. So far as he is guilty the victim must bear his
own burden.

The assertion that members of society are responsible
for one another's actions is in fact seen to owe its plausibility largely to a literal interpretation of rhetorical or
elliptical expressions. A proneness to think of society as
some entity other than its individual members may also
be detected in the passage just quoted. This cannot be
too severely condemned.[1]

In further indication of the kind of confusion on which
the notion of a shared responsibility thrives let me touch
on one other matter. But here we do not seem to be on
the track of a confusion as pernicious and widespread
as the ones we have considered.

The concern which a man has for his neighbour, and
especially for those who are intimately related to him,
has a very deep significance in regard to moral well-being.
A father is involved in the evil-doing of his son, not

---

[1] The topic is admirably treated by P. W. Ward in his *Sovereignty*
and by J. D. Mabbot in 'The Concepts of Politics,' *Mind*, July, 1938.

merely in the sense with which we have been mainly concerned, namely that the life of the son may indicate a culpable neglect on the part of a parent, but also in the sense that the bad life of a son is usually a profound tragedy for the parent. In this sense the parent bears in his inmost soul the sins of his children. Their virtues, on the other hand, will be the supreme joy and crown of his life. The more we are induced to think of one another in the light of Christ's revelation of the brotherhood of men, the more we shall find ourselves to be, *in this sense*, involved in the sins of others. No one who is morally sensitive could wish to dissociate himself from the moral attainment of others or wish to be spared the pain which is often the price of this supreme human relationship. But this, albeit crucial for a true view of divine and human relationships, is an entirely different matter from partaking of the guilt of another. We simply cannot in the latter way be wounded for the transgressions of others, we cannot at this point bear one another's burdens. And that is also, I believe, a truth of the very highest importance for a proper understanding of the individual's ultimate significance and destiny. We must not allow it to be obscured by misrepresenting the way in which, as we have just noted, it is possible for us to be involved in the sins of others.

An equation of the latter involvement with a sharing of responsibility reduces itself to absurdity in one very special way. For it is to God that men stand in the completest and most intimate relationship. And God would thus be involved in the sins of the world, not in the sense normally intended in Christian doctrines, but in the sense of being himself morally evil. I am not aware of a theory that has the boldness to countenance that blasphemy.

It is, indeed, sometimes said that God *accepts* responsibility for evil.[1] And the assertion may not be without

[1] Leonard Hodgson, *The Doctrine of the Trinity*, p. 117.

much significance *in a certain context*. But it certainly is not true in the sense that God shares the wickedness of man. Responsibility just cannot be accepted in that sense. It just is not transferable. We do indeed speak rather loosely of a Prime Minister accepting responsibility for his cabinet, of a friend becoming responsible for the debts of his neighbour, a parent for the actions of his children. But we know quite well that we speak metaphorically here. The Prime Minister is prepared to be treated as though he had endorsed the political action of a colleague even in a case where he has in fact opposed it or, in some instances, where it has been carried out without his knowledge. But we never really suppose that a Prime Minister *becomes* a foolish or mischievous person in those cases. On the contrary we think the better of him for loyalty to a colleague or party, or for putting the requirements of cabinet government before personal prestige and security of office. We believe this no less firmly when we proceed to oppose his administration on the basis of his readiness to have his cabinet treated as a single body —the procedure which political expediency normally requires. The only way in which the act of a colleague can reflect directly on the worth of his superior is by the act of the superior himself in choosing and maintaining him, or in cloaking his wickedness for personal reasons. No official of any kind can take over the actual wickedness of another, or, being good himself, lift the guilt from other shoulders to his own. It is not within anyone's power to *accept* responsibility in that sense. No one *becomes* good or evil by the act of another; if our metaphor suggests that it is possible for God, then the sooner we discard it in every context the better.

There is, no doubt, much that should be added to exhibit to the full the implications of the idea of a shared responsibility. But I believe that I have touched on the main causes of its persistence. And I must here reaffirm the conviction on which I must take my stand in the final analysis, namely that it is evident, as an immediate assurance of the moral consciousness, and thus independently of any kind of argument, that no person can be responsible for the action of another. The problem of freedom in general presents many difficulties. It is, as I have said, the hardest, as it is also the most crucial, of all ethical problems. But so far as the present issue is concerned there does not seem to be any real room for doubt. It would be more reasonable to surrender the notion of responsibility altogether than to seek to preserve it in so objectionable and distorted a form as that which declares guilt to be common.

We have here the support, not merely of the 'ordinary man of common sense' whose prestige is rightly very high in ethics, but also of far the greatest bulk of more reflective ethical thinking. The philosopher and the common man find themselves in almost complete accord here. If, therefore, theological theories contravene what seems to be so indisputable an ethical principle, and in some way or another the great bulk of them have done so from the time of St. Augustine to the present day, the onus of extricating themselves from a peculiar strait without impugning man's powers and judgment altogether, lies mainly on the theologian. But the situation as a whole is of the greatest concern to the moralist as well.

We must beware especially of desperate attempts to break out of this impasse by sheer intellectual violence. Dr. Whale, after stressing the idea of 'mass sinfulness' which he does not hesitate to accept, and having declared that our lives "interlock to form an organic system of evil," hastens to add that "personal responsibility and freedom are the essence of what we mean by moral personality."[1] How are these statements to be reconciled? The only answer attempted is that there can be no answer because "Sin, like freedom, is by hypothesis inexplicable."[2] This is a peculiarly ill-founded exploitation of the 'inexplicable' character of sin and freedom. For they are inexplicable precisely because they cannot enter into a system—'organic' or otherwise. It is just the aspect in which it is inexplicable, not merely in terms of scientific prediction which Whale has mainly in mind, but in any terms, that precludes any notion of mass sinfulness and the assumptions about the origin of sin which the author confidently endorses.

[1] Christian Doctrine, p. 46.   [2] *Op. cit.*, p. 49.

CHAPTER VII

PRIMITIVE ATTITUDES

Behind the assumptions and the positions with which we have been mainly concerned in this essay there lies the failure to distinguish effectively between such judgments as we may pass on the outward course of conduct and the appraisement of the properly moral worth of the agent. To this I have already alluded. It can readily be seen how the unrefined morality that looks no further than external effects carries with it the ascription to all concerned in the production of those effects of a general responsibility for them. The combination of these procedures in recent religious thought, has a special significance in relation to the general reversion to primitive attitudes that has been so dismal a feature of recent history.

In primitive life the group is the essential unit, and not the individual. Private property as we know it is rare. There is little scope for initiative, even the rulers or 'judges' (as they would then be in most cases) being heavily circumscribed in their activities by the more inexorable rule of immemorial custom. There is a clear pattern for all behaviour from the simplest to the most important tasks. And where consciousness of individual worth and distinctness is so little developed, the misdeeds of particular members of a tribe or nation, as well as noble actions on their part, are accounted to the community at large. To it belongs the glory of achievement, it feels pride or shame, as the case may be, it is the real bearer of guilt.

This is very familiar ground to historians, and the tale has been told so well and so fully that it would be idle to embroider it here. But, if required, abundant illustrations could be adduced without going further than familiar parts of the Scripture. Among the most celebrated is the story of Achan.[1] When his treachery was discovered both he *and his family* were barbarously done to death in the Valley of Achor. The dealings of God with his people were often interpreted in the same way. The sins of the fathers were visited on the children to the third and the fourth generation. The righteous, on the other hand, would be rewarded especially in the prosperity of his seed, and the lives of the godly were an assurance of mercy, 'the sure mercies of David,' to be invoked in the petitions of all. God was above all the God of Israel, and it was in his regard for the nation as a whole that his righteousness was shown. It was the seeming suspension of this general providence that caused the greatest bewilderment, and when the more wayward facts of history were hard to compress into this mould, the Jews continued to nurse the 'unconquerable hope' of the eventual fulfilment of God's promise to the people. It is well known that the idea of a personal immortality had far less prominence in Hebrew thought than used to be supposed.[2]

Along with this identification of the individual with his community, the thought and practice of primitive peoples, as of those civilizations that have least extricated themselves from primitive habits of mind, is also marked by indifference to motive and purpose startling to more enlightened ages. A taboo has been broken, that is enough; retribution and expiation must follow. This was one of the main causes of tribal feuds and the perpetuation of these in wars which were, as it happens, an important

[1] Joshua vii. 18-26.

[2] Cf. H. Wheeler Robinson, *The Religious Ideas of the Old Testament*, pp. 91-101.

factor in the rise of civilization. Early wars were rarely wars of aggression. They were the natural expression of the morality of 'an eye for an eye' which, being too external and mechanical to find amelioration in a change of heart and amicable understanding, perpetuated its ruthless logic in accepted and hardening enmities as retribution and retaliation continued their bloody alternation from one age to another.

Even in the ordering of society to-day we are left with a nest of problems engendered in this way. For prejudices die hard and are easily inflamed. And the attitudes we have noted have a way of persisting in subtle forms in the outlook of more enlightened times. How much so can be well illustrated from the study of Greek thought and practice. Let one example suffice here. Among Aristotle's celebrated criticisms of Plato's theory of communism is the following. If a member of Plato's ruling class, as between whom there would be a complete communism of wives and children, killed another of that class he might unwittingly be killing an actual parent or blood relation. He would thus, so Aristotle concludes, in fact be guilty of a crime much more hideous than mere murder—parricide having a very special grimness for the Greeks—a crime from which he might well have recoiled were the circumstances plain to him. Aristotle here takes no account of the fact that there would be no knowledge of the relationship or intention of the crime in its fulness as parricide. The proneness of the Greeks to identify the good man with the good citizen and to limit their loyalties to their own city, is also a truism in the interpretation of Greek life.

But not only do these primitive attitudes continue to exercise a subtle influence on subsequent practice, they are also apt to return, made worse by the distortions of sophistication, in periods of confusion and distress.

This has been one of the most serious tragedies of the twentieth century. A combination of forces has thrown the world into such turmoil as to provide an unusual opportunity for the recrudescence of those primitive impulses and reactions to which men are not wholly immune even in the most civilized communities in times of crisis. The morality of the tribe reasserts itself.

This appears in its most lurid and extravagant forms in countries where enlightenment is a late arrival, or where progress and civilization have been restricted in scope and retarded by powerful reactionary forces. The measure of a country's privation must also be put in the reckoning when we consider its reversion to barbaric attitudes and standards. But there is hardly a country in the Western world to-day whose civilization is not somewhat stained by the return of an outmoded undiscriminating ethic.

One peculiarly significant example of this reversion to barbarism is the persecution of the Jews. There are, indeed, many facets to this strange aberration. But conspicuous among them is the delusion, sincere enough in many cases, that the Jews are fair game, that they have incurred some kind of perpetual outlawry by the guilt in which they are steeped as a race through the ill deeds of particular members of that race, sometimes more, sometimes less, remote; some counts go back two thousand years and should, one would expect, have been atoned for by now, if the need be allowed, by the sufferings of one generation of Jews after another and their humiliating segregation in ghettos and hideouts—a fate that was bound to sear the soul of the victims and add its own complications to the tasks of posterity. It is the same resurgence of a tribal ethos that induces a people to seek its greatness solely in some legendary glory of its heroes unrelated to the true enrichment of national life as a whole and induced artificially and, mainly, through the depression of those peoples themselves. A barbarism of this kind takes the course we expect in that exclusiveness by which the countries that are most completely in the grip of a distorted nationalism deny to other nations, and especially to the reviled lower races, privileges which they have no hesitation in arrogating to themselves. But this resurgence of primitive morality, grosser as we have stressed because it is appearing among civilized and gifted peoples, is by no means restricted to the countries whose recent record is most stained by cruelties and oppression. For the countries that have banded together, as upholders of democracy, in opposition to the countries that would have involved the rest of the world in their own disorders, have been themselves infected by the ills they set out to cure. In our turn, we are ourselves prone to regard the German nation as a whole as steeped in some kind of collective guilt, and the reckoning is again, in some quarters, taken back many centuries. The 'Germans' have committed certain crimes, and to be a German, it is thought, is tantamount to implication in them. These attitudes often take their shape without much attention to such questions as what do we mean by a nation or the 'Germans,' what part have particular individuals taken in the promotion of national policy, what opposition has there been, and what complicating factors, and in particular how far could individuals have made their will effective and how far were they in the grip of political and social systems which they could not have properly foreseen and averted. Considerations of the kind suggested by these questions would certainly mitigate moral blame, and, in some cases, completely exonerate from it. Failure to take account of them sets democracy on the road that leads to fascism.

This does not mean that we are not to treat aggressive nations on a collective basis. It would be wholly impossible in Germany to-day to deal with each individual strictly according to his merits. Neither is it suggested that we can set aside the unity and continuity of political entities by treating the Germany of to-day without regard to the Germany of the recent past. That way lie those seemingly innocent delusions that we now know to be so pregnant with tragic possibilities. The new education of Germany, in its broader aspects, will have many a hard fact to bring home to the German people; there will require to be awakened a new understanding of the kind of world in which we live to-day and a profounder and more intelligent sense of the social responsibilities of all. And these are clearly not lessons to be taught in the class-room alone. Reality is the great school-master here, and there must be no sheltering from the experiences by which its schooling proceeds. To forget the course of history and dissociate men from their environment in our treatment of them is to relapse into that abstract individualism in whose condemnation we have fully concurred. But whatever the measures which a realistic view of the facts as a whole may require, and whatever concessions may have to be made to measures of expediency or those devices, of which the greatest is government, by which fallible creatures must deal with situations which they can never fully understand, the administration of justice must not be complicated by the ascription to men of a genuine moral guilt which is not in proportion to their own deliberate betrayal of their ideals.

I have heard it argued that a person of German nationality who opposed the Nazi régime from the start and continued to do so at the cost of great suffering to himself and his family, would still be a sharer in the common guilt of the German people for aggression and cruelties perpetrated under the Nazi régime. And this, in fact, seems to me the only position which it is consistent for anyone who believes in collective responsibility to hold. It is the *reductio ad absurdum* of that belief. For it shows that its adherents are no longer thinking about ethics in a civilized way.

An inverted form of the same relapse into primitive ethical attitudes regards opposition to the enactments of one's own community as invariably an evil of the greatest magnitude. Although 'the Germans' were embarked on a career of violence and destruction, the resistance which would be proper, and a supreme duty, in members of other nations would, it appears, be an abomination on the part of a German. As Dr. Ewing observes: "The very people who clamour most for punishment on the whole German nation sometimes absurdly blame the German refugees on the ground that they ought not to have deserted their country, however badly she behaved."[1] It is on the same principle, so far as I can make out, that Pastor Niemoller offered his services to Hitler in a naval capacity at the outset of the war. This attitude finds some support in the confusion to which we alluded in Chapter II, the fallibility of the individual being thought to commit him to complete reliance on the wisdom of his community. But when that attitude is carried in actual practice to the extremes we have instanced it does not seem possible to ascribe it wholly, or even mainly, to confusion of thought. It is an infection of feeling by the ethics of the tribe, the upwelling of a barbarous strain not yet eradicated by culture and enlightenment.

It will perhaps be interjected at this point that philosophy has not an altogether clean bill in regard to the trends we have noticed. This would not be without

[1] 'The ethics of punishing Germany,' *Hibbert Journal*, January, 1945, p. 101.

some foundation. For idealist philosophy, especially in its most uncompromising forms, tended towards a social and political absolutism in which the individual was submerged and lost. The notion of the State as a vague superstructure somehow above and beyond the lives of its individual members owed the wide currency that it had at a certain period largely to the teaching of idealists (using this ambiguous term here in its technical philosophical sense). This, in great measure, was due to faults which idealism shared with the individualism to which it claimed to supply the corrective. For both extremes depend in the last resort on a highly abstract view of the individual. For the simplification which consists in minimizing the dependence of man on society, and the consequent negative view of the function of the State, idealism substituted that simplification by which incompatibility of interests and disparities of view are finally swallowed in the absolute unity of the social will—from which there is no appeal. We do not require a close analysis to allow that certain types of idealist theory encouraged the notion of the all-inclusive absolute State and that worship of the State as an end in itself which developed on the Continent, and especially in Germany, in the nineteenth century. But it must also be stressed that the idealists themselves were acutely aware of the dangers of their view; while they had no doubt about the finality of idealist solutions to great human problems they had a very deep regard for individual freedom and the varieties by which corporate life is enriched, and they sought to do justice to them in their doctrines. Nor is this altogether a strain. For the individual has for them his importance as a finite centre, even if he is also prone to lose his distinctness[1]

[1] On this aspect of idealist philosophy see 'Life and Finite Individuality,' *Proceedings of the Aristotelian Society*, Supplementary Volume, 1918.

in the Absolute. Idealism is a many sided philosophy, and Hegel, who is normally regarded as the arch culprit in this context, and who was in fact driven, both by his natural sympathies and the exigencies of theoretical consistency, to some authoritarian extremes, has also a great deal to teach us about the function of minor or non-political associations within the State and about the freedom of the individual.[1] Other idealists put a considerable strain on strict idealist theory in their anxiety not to put freedom in jeopardy. The precise relation of idealism to the rise of despotic practices has yet to be properly investigated, and it is certainly a subject which should have early attention. At present we are only too prone to make unbalanced and ill-considered generalizations about it. But it does not require expert knowledge to show that the influence of idealism on the kind of authoritarianism which has been an all too common and tragic spectacle in Europe to-day has been much exaggerated and distorted by superficial critics of idealism and incautious historians. The great idealist thinkers would certainly have been quite horrified themselves to witness the progeny they are supposed to have fathered. And when every allowance has been made for that dynamic of ideas which their originators could not have foreseen and controlled, the count against idealist philosophy in regard to the lapses of the twentieth century remains very meagre on the whole. Idealism drew its inspiration from too rational a culture to make it, even at some removes, the philosophy of barbarism.

Theology does not come off so lightly. For the tones in which it speaks most unmistakably to-day, and, it must be admitted, those which echo most clearly its traditions in the past, find a responsive chord more easily in the

[1] Cf. T. M. Knox, 'Hegel and Prussianism,' *Philosophy*, January, 1940.

primitive mentality induced, as we have seen, by confusion and stress, than in the cultural and scientific advances of our age. Having failed to make commensurate progress with the latter and to respond effectively to the peculiar opportunity and challenge of the present time, it allies itself with the starker forces of reaction, the affinity being especially direct in the repudiation of that most treasured and significant feature of civilized life, the sense of personal responsibility. To this the 'Theology of Crisis' owes much of its appeal, for in addition to the general reluctance to leave the security of established ideas and live at the adventurous spiritual level which is possible to-day, there is also the explosive emotional power with which an eruption of elemental forces into the crisis of an age of enlightenment is bound to be charged. The claims, made especially by the Continental theologians to have produced a 'preacher's theology' depends in part, though by no means wholly,[1] on the measure in which they are able to turn the emotional disturbances attendant on the more reactionary factors in the world crisis to the advantage of their doctrine. Some have gone very far in that direction, and this unholy alliance with the forces of reaction is a most distressing, as it is also a most ominous, feature of religious thought at the present time. Let us look at it more closely.

[1] See below, Chapter XII.

CHAPTER VIII

THEOLOGY AND REACTION

As has been observed, the affinity of the New Theology with some reactionary trends is seen most plainly in the notion of a shared responsibility. Strictly speaking the theological view of universal sinfulness does not allow of the limitation of responsibility to the community to which the agent belongs. It is not properly a group responsibility. But this is a nicety which goes unregarded for the most part. For group responsibility and the doctrine of universal guilt are at one in their opposition to the notion of individual guilt incurred by deliberate betrayal of principle. The affinity is more marked than the differences, and theological writers, in point of fact, refer extensively to the collectivist trend in the temper and practice of recent years in support of traditionalist doctrines.

Consider next the attitude adopted by the churches most deeply committed to these doctrines, especially in their more uncompromising forms, towards the course of social and political events. It is common in this reference to instance the heroic resistance of the German Lutheran Churches to the Nazi régime in rebuttal of any accusation of political ineptitude or sloth or the absence of a progressive understanding suited to the needs of a democratic age. It is they, apparently, who have stood in the van of resistance to evil and reactionary forces. It is they who have held up the banner of freedom with the greatest persistence in the face of the relentless tyranny of the State and the indifference of the masses. Theirs was the only resistance sufficiently dynamic to survive the organized ruthlessness of Hitlerism, and from them accordingly will come the power and vision for the creative tasks of the reconstituted democracies. Such at least are the asseverations frequently made, made with a great show of confidence but not invariably from quarters with any peculiar claim to be well informed about recent and current affairs. Before we endorse them there is much that we need to consider.

Firstly, it is by no means true that effective resistance has been confined to the Confessional Church. Its struggle was never so solitary as some of its admirers are apt to conclude. Reluctant though we may feel to stint any part of our praise for those who have passed through trials rarely equalled in the annals of persecution, fairness requires that we acknowledge also the courage of others who partook of their suffering and mounted to similar heights of heroic endurance. Among these were members of Protestant bodies other than the Confessional Church, and notable Catholic leaders such as the redoubtable Bishop von Galen and Cardinal Faulhaber. And along with these must be reckoned also a great array of eminent scientists, scholars and men of letters. Many of these professed no religious belief of any kind, but the record of their endurance can hardly be dimmed by that fact. Finally, the count must also include numberless common folk who neither by gift of leadership nor any other eminence, nor by the grimness of their endurance, will break into the pages of history, those who have 'no memorial; who are perished as though they had never been' but whose righteousness hath not been forgotten. There does not seem to have been a monopoly of suffering and endurance in Nazi Germany. And the extent to which the Lutheran Church was the focus of resistance is far from established.

It can, I think, be admitted that Lutheran and Neo-Calvinist theology has an authentic dynamic power that is almost unique in the world to-day. And an attempt will be made to lay bare its secret before we close. But the question we have to determine at the moment is whether the involvement of that theology in reactionary movements and the murkiness of its ethical thinking preclude its being turned to a direction that is really progressive and creative. And in spite of a natural anxiety to be ungrudging in acknowledging such part as the Lutheran Church has played in the struggle against Hitlerism, we must not fail also to remark the very special nature of the resistance it offered, and the strict limitation of its scope. For that was not in the main a political or social resistance in the sense of concerning itself with social injustice and oppression in general. It was at the point where Hitlerism touched the activities of the Confessional Church itself in matters of doctrine and worship that the latter began, somewhat belatedly, to manifest a sensitive conscience towards the savagery of the Nazi régime. And, on some readings, the Confessional Church continued in the main to acquiesce with an altogether surprising equanimity in acts of brutality and terror and general misgovernment which ought to have aroused immediate revulsion and protest in any Christian body.

But this is less strange when we turn to the actual teaching of the leaders of the Confessional Church in regard to the relation of Church and State. Witness the fulsome, almost blasphemous, reverence of the State in a celebrated pamphlet on *Church and State* by Barth. The author is loth to withhold the aura of a divine sanction even from the vilest acts of the State. An annoying allusiveness of style does not obscure the conviction that "the State cannot lose the honour that is its due. For that very reason the New Testament ordains that in all circumstances

---

[1] Cf. correspondence in the *Spectator*, June, 1945.

honour must be shown to its representatives."[1] "The very State which is 'demonic' may will evil, and yet, in an outstanding way, may be constrained to do good."[2] When Pilate released Barabbas and delivered Jesus to scurging and crucifixion "this extremely unjust human judge" was "by this very act of political authority . . . fulfilling the word of the supremely just Divine Judge."[3] There is much ambiguity in the presentation of these views, and especially a failure to note properly the distinction between that direct ethical sanction of legal enactment which is due to the inherent rightfulness of a law, and that indirect sanction of a particular law because obedience to it is part of a maintenance of government which proves to be on the whole beneficial. But the general drift of the argument is plain. There is no unambiguous condemnation of social injustice such as would warrant the interference and opposition of the Church. And the point that stands out by the emphasis it receives is the overwhelming importance of 'intercession.' "Christians are called to offer 'supplications, prayers, intercessions and thanksgiving' for all men, and in particular for Kings and all who are in positions of authority."[4] When the power of the State "has been perverted what greater service can we render than that of intercession."[5] This service, it is also affirmed, includes all others, and if intercession were really understood in a way which included continuous constructive criticism and interference, there would be no very serious ground of complaint although the ambiguous statement and a misplaced emphasis might properly elicit a protest. But in fact there is no hint that the church should concern itself at all in matters of government, much less withhold its obedience, *except at one point.*

[1] *Op. cit.*, p. 18.   [2] *Op. cit.*, p. 17.   [3] *Op. cit.*, p. 18.
[4] *Op. cit.*, p. 62.   [5] *Op. cit.*, p. 69.

That is the point at which the State interferes with "the freedom to preach justification."[1] Even here the admission of the right to resist is somewhat tardy. The following passage is I think worth quoting in full.

"The power of the State, on its side, may become guilty of opposition to the Lord of Lords, to that divine ordinance to which it owes its power. If Christians are still to respect the State, even then, their docility in this instance can only be passive, and, as such, limited. The 'subjection' can in no case mean that the church and its members will approve, and wish of their own free will to further, the claims and undertakings of the State, if once the State power is turned not to the protection but to the suppression of the preaching of justification. Even then Christians will never fail to grant that which is indispensable to the State power as guardian of the public law, as an ordained power—tribute to whom tribute is due, custom to whom custom, fear to whom fear, honour to whom (as representative and bearer of ἐξουσία) honour—even if the State abuses this ἐξουσία, and demonstrates its opposition, as a demonic power, to the Lord of Lords. Even then, according to Matthew xxii. 21, Christians will render unto Cæsar the things which are Cæsar's, i.e. whatever is his due, not as a good or a bad Cæsar, but simply as Cæsar; the right which is his, even if he turns that right to wrong. As has been shown it is and remains a God-established ἐξουσία, and that which we owe it, even then, must not be withheld."[2]

In this way, very cautiously, Barth leads to the admission that Christians cannot "take upon themselves responsibility for those intentions and undertakings of the State which directly or indirectly are aimed against the freedom of preaching. Of course it must be understood that even then the 'subjection' will not cease. But their

[1] *Op. cit.*, p. 71.　　　　[2] *Op. cit.*, p. 67.

submission, their *respect* for the power of the State to which they continue to give what they owe, will consist in becoming its victims, who, in their concrete action will not accept any responsibility, who cannot inwardly co-operate, and who *as* 'subjects' will be unable to conceal the fact, and indeed ought to express it publicly, in order that the preaching of justification may be continued under all circumstances. All this will be done, not *against* the State, but as the Church's service *for* the State. Respect for the authority of the State is indeed an annexe to the priestly function of the Church towards the State. Christians would be neglecting the distinctive service which they can and must render to the State, were they to adopt an attitude of unquestioning assent to the will and action of the State, which is directly or indirectly aimed at the suppression of the freedom of the Word of God. For the possibility of intercession for the State stands or falls with the freedom of God's Word."[1]

"For the sake of the freedom to preach justification the Church expects that the State will be a true State, and thus that it will create and administer justice. But the Church honours the State even when this expectation is not fulfilled."[2] The true exercise of this freedom is also held in one passage to require 'corresponding work'[3] and the 'democratic conception of the State' is allowed, again very cautiously, to be "a justifiable expansion of the thought of the New Testament."[4] But this incidental admission does not make it at all plain whether the Church itself should relate its own message directly to social and political enactment, and what sort of resistance it can properly offer to evil political systems. Shrouding his own view behind the vague insistence that "true scriptural preaching and teaching" and "the true and scriptural

[1] *Op. cit.*, p. 69.   [2] *Op. cit.*, p. 71.
[3] *Op. cit.*, p. 79.   [4] *Op. cit.*, p. 80.

administration of the sacraments" include "everything that the Church can render to the State, even all the political obligations of its members,"[1] Barth continues the plea, which appears to be his only important concern, that "the Church must have freedom to proclaim divine justification."[2] This is moreover the test of political justice at every point. "The State will realize its own potentialities, and thus will be a just State, in proportion as it not merely positively allows, but actively grants, this freedom to the Church."[3] The notion of some more direct and independent criterion of State enactment such as 'natural law' is summarily dismissed. "The State is called to establish human law, and it has the capacity to do so. We cannot measure what this law is by any Romantic or Liberalistic idea of 'natural law,' but simply by the concrete law of freedom, which the Church must claim for its Word, so far as it is the Word of God." And it is, therefore, clear that "by proclaiming divine justification it [the Church] will be rendering the best possible assistance to the establishment and maintenance of human justice and law."[5] "This is what the Church has to offer to the State when, on its side, it desires from the State nothing but freedom."[6]

Prevarication over the meaning of this 'freedom' and the suggestion that the State in which it is properly enjoyed will also attain to the fullest justice through the Christian living of its members does not hide the failure to indicate any positive political duty of the Church itself, or of Christians individually (they remain "foreigners in the sphere of the State"),[7] much less to admit, and to confront squarely, the problem how the Church,

---

[1] *Op. cit.*, p. 83.   [2] *Op. cit.*, p. 83.   [4] *Op. cit.*, p. 83.

[4] *Op. cit.*, p. 84.   [5] *Op. cit.*, p. 82.   [6] *Op. cit.*, p. 85.

[7] *Op. cit.*, p. 80.

officially or in the private conduct of its members, should conduct itself in communities where the freedom to 'preach justification' has not in fact arrested the commission of great injustices, supported by barbarous atrocities.

The 'freedom to preach justification'—in other words, the freedom of the Church to go about its own business, very mindful of the fact that its members are 'foreigners in the sphere of the State'—indicates the point at which the Church must take serious cognisance of political activities. This is entirely in keeping with the limited and belated resistance of the Lutheran Church to the Nazi régime. When the State sets itself up as God, when it intrudes upon acts of worship and directs them to its own purposes or pollutes the teaching of the Church with its own propaganda, then, and *then only* is the Church to make a stand. There seems every reason to believe that this represents fairly the attitude adopted in practice for the most part by the Confessional Church in Germany.

It is also entirely in keeping with the general trend of Protestant thought in Germany. The emphasis has been throughout upon the separation between Church and State expressed in the maxim of Frederick the Great—anticipated as Barth observes[1] in Calvin's *Institutio*—*Suum Cuique*. This is the view expressed in Luther's advice to the rebellious peasants, and subsequently in Calvin's counsel of despair to those who are "cruelly vexed by an inhuman prince"—"it is not for us to remedy these evils"[2]—combined with the incitement to disobedience when the princes "seek to tear God from his throne," and, latterly, in the quietism and isolationism of the main Protestant bodies in the Germany of very recent

[1] *Op. cit.*, p. 85.
[2] *Institutes*, Book IV, Chapter XX.

years. To illustrate the contentions of this passage in detail would take us far afield, but I do not think it will be seriously disputed that the aloofness of the Church from practical affairs and its preoccupation with a spiritual message, as expressed in the pamphlet to which I have referred, represents the course pursued, with little deviation or dissent, by the Lutheran Churches from the days of their founder to the present time. The affirmation of the principle by which their course was shaped is to-day more emphatic and explicit than it has sometimes been, but it has rarely been sufficiently subdued to make a substantial difference to practice. Nor have autocratic powers been slow in the past to avail themselves of the cloak which it offers to oppression and misrule. Such reproaches as the Church might presume to make were put out of court by its own doctrines. And, without attempting to estimate the relative importance of the various factors that led to confusion and savagery in Germany between the two wars, we can clearly see, in the impotence and blindness of the German Protestant Churches in the early years of Hitlerism, and their bewilderment and fury when at last appeasement left little but themselves to devour, the working out of the logic of their doctrines to a more calamitous and significant consequence than anything approached in the past. In the subsequent humiliation and sufferings of the Confessional Churches themselves the nemesis of their own teaching is visible to all.

There could be no clearer exhibition of that essential inadequacy of the Reformation to which we have already alluded. The earlier celebrated doctrine of the 'two swords,' deeply rooted as it was in the mediæval dichotomy of the spiritual and the secular, comes to life in the Protestant teaching which adheres most consistently to the absorption of individual morality in a cosmic drama (consistency here being an outstanding merit of Barthian-ism) in the shape of a much sharper cleavage between Church and State, with the resulting elevation of the latter, than was ever conceived in medi-eval times—and without the restraint of Natural Law.

But it is not merely by giving a despotic power its head in consequence of the religious isolationism we have just noted that Protestant thought in Germany fanned the flames of reactionary movements. We have already observed how that notion of inevitable sinfulness which calls for the gross elevation of the State, as the instrument of secular order, together with the relegation of spiritual life and religious thought to a sphere of its own, in Barthian terms the 'separation of justice from justification,' involves the same depreciation of the individual which is the most baneful feature of the Nazi myths about Blood and Race and *Volk*. On this score we need only reiterate here what should require little emphasis for any who can read the lesson of our times at all, that there can be no more certain deflation of the sense of individual value and the dignity of personal life than the abrogation of individual responsibility in the properly moral sense. To weaken the sense of individual worth in this particular way is very plainly to play into the hands of irresponsible totalitarian régimes.

But, further, in order to sustain the doctrine of the guilt in which all men are steeped through the fall, it is thought necessary to postulate such an alienation of man from God as to veil the nature of God altogether from the eyes of man. For the sinner there can be no natural knowledge of God, there is no normal channel by which the Divine can communicate with us. Hence the mysterious act of grace, the triumphant victory of Christ by which the power of sin is broken and the absolute Word of God finds lodgment in human souls. The unique

Christian revelation, by the channel of the Scriptures, is the only beam that can lighten our darkness, it is wholly mysterious, and will remain an insoluble enigma express-ible only in paradox and antinomy. To seek some analogy of religious truth in human experience, to endeavour to draw near to God of our own accord rather than despair utterly and wholly of ourselves, and of all human powers, is to fall into that sinful self-assertion and unbelief which is the very core of evil and a sure means of perdition. By faith alone, faith that is a wholly irrational leap in the dark, is man's soul illumined and saved.

This doctrine is in part a reaction against attempts to bring reality entirely within the compass of our own minds, either by way of naturalism or by certain forms of pantheism or by idealistic attempts to present the ultimate unity of the universe in completely rational terms. Of these idealism had the greatest attraction for Christian thinkers in the last century. But it is open to serious metaphysical objections, and the claim that reality has a character not expressible in rational terms has been vigorously pressed in recent years. In religious thought this leads to stress on the supra-rational character of God, a view to which Otto—incidentally, a figure of much greater permanent importance than Barth (or any of his satellites)—has given remarkable expression in his *Idea of the Holy*. The new emphasis on the transcendent nature of God is exceptionally timely. It supplies a corrective to religious thought that brings it out of many shoals and shallows. But the presentation of it, and in particular the attempt to posit and deal with the extremely difficult question to which it gives rise, namely what is the relation of a supreme transcendent reality to the course of human experience, is hopelessly confused by entanglement with the traditionalist doctrine of the fall. It is one of the main weaknesses of Barthian Theology that little attempt is made to relate the view of man's alienation from God through the fall to such objections as are made on general grounds to idealism and kindred theories. The upshot of this is a contempt of human powers in general together with such an irresponsible and bewildering indulgence in paradox as to put a veritable premium on sheer unreason. This also plays very effectively into the hands of reaction.

These warnings take a very grim and substantial form when we consider the relation of Protestant thought in Hitlerite Germany to religious movements of a frankly pagan and distorted character. Accessions to the latter have proceeded with a significant ease of transition. This may be seen very strikingly in the drift towards avowedly pagan positions in the case of Friedrich Gogarten.

Gogarten[1] reverted to the Lutheran doctrine of the 'orders.' But, sharing the pessimism of Barth in regard to all human endeavour, and, at the same time, dismayed at the lack of any principle of practice other than the injunction to eschew worldly wisdom altogether and rely on the Bible and prayer, he arrived at the view that the secular order of the State was the final arbiter in ethical matters. There was thus to be a sharp separation of the 'Kingdom of the Gospel' from the 'Kingdom of the Law.' With the rise of Hitlerism Gogarten substituted the *Volk* or Nation for the State as the ultimate ethical standard.

The wheel comes full circle in the undisguised paganism of the German Faith Movement. This religion, with its idolatrous confession, 'Blood and Honour,' owes much to the teaching of Rosenberg, author of the celebrated *Myth of the Twentieth Century*. Proceeding on the assumption that different religions suit different times and peoples, it is urged that the Germans must worship God in a

[1] His principle work has the significant title, *Politische Ethik*.

Nordic way.[1] This is the opposite to the Semitic style. It lays the emphasis on freedom and honour rather than on sin and guilt, it has none of the submissiveness, the 'grovelling before God,' thought to typify Hebrew religion. On this count it claims affinity with liberal theology, but the resemblance is very superficial. For the critical attitude towards the Old Testament is very different in the two cases. And, in spite of a contemptuous attitude towards the Old Testament, what we have in large part in the German Faith Movement is a reversion to the more tribal features of Old Testament thought— with the substitution of the Germans for the Jews. An attempt to bring this within the framework of a Christian view is made by Emmanuel Hirsch,[2] and the German Christian Party. Repudiating the relativism of the German Faith Movement, Hirsch acknowledges the final authority of the Gospel. But the truth of the Gospel concerns only our eternal destiny. For guidance in the storms and stresses of the present life we must listen to the voice of God in those events themselves. This means in practice conformity to the forces by which society is swayed at a particular time, the right of a group to dominate the individual receiving special emphasis. Such extravagant attempts to combine Christianity with Aryanism and to present Nazi mythology in the guise of an up-to-date Christian view hardly deserve serious attention in themselves. Detailed description would certainly fall outside our purpose. But their appearance in Germany, and especially the extent to which they drew their general support and leadership from among members of Protestant Churches, is most significant. For it will be clear how much this has been facilitated by the proneness

[1] See Wilhelm Hauer: *Deutscher Gottschau.*

[2] See his *Deutsches Volkstum und der evangelische Glaube* and *Der Weg der Theologie.*

of Lutheran thought to absorb the distinctively ethical life and its principles into a unique religious experience. Such teaching, in combination with a collectivist view of responsibility, and the denunciation of reason, left members of Christian congregations very helpless in the swirling tides of the Nazi Movement. It explains an otherwise bewildering susceptibility to delusion.

As the late A. E. Garvie put the matter: "The dualism of Lutheran theology, which separated the realm of grace from the social order, and held each to be autonomous under God as Redeemer and as Creator has made it possible for Christians in Germany to acquiesce in policies which the Christian conscience would otherwise condemn."[1]

Small wonder that Barth himself should have been so violent in his denunciation of any modification of his view in the direction of a theory of orders.[2] For while modification of his view is inevitable if religion is not to be divorced from life altogether, such modification only exposes the more effectively the calamitous results of following his lead. It hinders the evasive shuffling between the extremes of his dualism.

[1] 'Features and Factors of the World Crisis,' *Hibbert Journal*, January, 1941, p. 31.

[2] See especially the celebrated *Nein! Antwort an Emil Brunner*.

CHAPTER IX

PESSIMISM

THE SPREAD OF LUTHERAN ideas in other countries than Germany has not been attended by such sinister consequences as in Germany itself. For, in other countries, these ideas have not as yet implanted themselves so deeply in the religious life of the community as a whole. The counteracting factors have also been stronger. But there have not been lacking of late ominous indications of the course which such doctrines as we have been discussing are likely to cut for themselves in the life of the more liberal countries of the West. Of these the most marked, I believe, is the spread of a perverse and cloying pessimism.

There is much for pessimism to feed on in the world to-day. It seems easier to pick a quarrel with life than at any time past. Wars and oppression, to say nothing of other ills, afford occasions for it rarely approached before. For they owe the peculiar hideousness that they wear to-day to those very advances which should have prevented their appearance altogether. There seems to be a sinister twist at the heart of things. So at least one might conclude if one judged hastily. But a calmer appraisal of the facts as a whole induces greater caution. For not only are the more dire and depressing ills that have befallen men to-day capable of a much kindlier explanation than that which ascribes them straightway to a sullen perverted rebellion against enlightenment itself, but a truly impartial survey might well find considerably more to admire in the actions of men to-day than there is to deplore. There have been senseless brutality, callousness, greed, a very lust for destruction; but there have also been heroism, endurance, self-denial, cheerfulness and humour in the grimmest hours of toil and suffering, a sense of companionship and a willingness to harness one's energies to a great cause. Idealism has had as good a run as despair. The horror and savagery have themselves been parasitic upon good. And if we turn from the good and ill in the nature and actions of men to examine the conditions in which we live to-day, while there are more deadly and terrifying engines of destruction than ever before, more effective organization for evil ends, the means of more absolute despotic rule, there are also more excellent remedies for ills of that kind. If we have the flame-thrower we have also penicillin, if we have the Spitfire we have also the collapsible dinghy, if we have the bombing plane we have swift evacuation of big cities, if we have the concentration camp we have the Red Cross, if there are deadlier guns and tanks there is also swift manœuvre which spares an army the decimation of its infantry in the trenches. Gas warfare seems of itself to have ousted gas warfare. And so the tale might continue. He would indeed be an insensitive soul who confessed to no dismay in the face of the destructive power that can be accumulated in the hands of an irresponsible minority to-day. And the ills that we suffer can not be lightly dismissed because we have at least partial remedies for them. But it seems also plain that if we take a truly comprehensive view, the world has in actual fact gained much more in amenities of various kinds and in organization for mutual support and help than it has lost in devices and systems that make for wretchedness. In the cultural as opposed to the more material sphere the odds seem most decidedly on the side of good. For the means that make a perverted propaganda successful is even more effective in extending the scope and influence of enlightenment and true education. Willy-nilly, the nations of the world are brought together, and understanding and sympathy break through the barriers of class and race. So that when the fullest count is taken of such evils as war, unemployment, malnutrition, and the ills that wait on these, it still seems possible to conclude that life on the whole is better for mankind than it has ever been before, and there are prospects of very substantial advances in a future not too remote, dimmed though these are also by the possibility of a complete disaster—if irrational-ism has its way. We can thus conclude, without any pretence at an exhaustive count, that an unrelieved pessimism or any settled gloominess of view has even less warrant than the exaggerated hopes of your facile optimist.

It is important that this should be established and kept steadily before our minds, not merely because a settled pessimism is an ill frame of mind in itself, but also because it saps the energies of men and misdirects their efforts. For the same reason it is especially necessary that, in our survey of the good and ill factors in modern life, we should not only make our count as comprehensive and fair as we can, but also that we should not be in too great a haste to ascribe such ills as men are heir to at present to a proportionate prevalence of evil design. There is much that requires consideration before the bearing of the social and international upheavals of the present age on properly moral qualities can be appraised. Much careful analysis is needed. And it is here that the spread of a sullen pessimism in Western countries bears most clearly on our discussion. For the prophets of it are only too prone to heap up the evils that afflict us, and lay them generally at the door of mankind. And the more completely our ills are equated in this way with moral evil the more radical and depressing they are. Dissension, brutality, war, these alone, it seems, give the measure of our moral stature, and we are invited to feast our minds upon their ill character, almost to the exclusion of other reflections, as a constant reminder of the extent to which we are in the power of moral evil.

This is carried, in the recent *Report of the Oxford Conference*—as considered and, presumably, as representative a statement as one could desire—to the point of presenting the war against evil in society as a struggle "against a destructive principle in the universe itself, and against superhuman powers of evil."[1] . . . "We cannot," it is urged, "in our own strength contend successfully against satanic powers." Some account is taken of natural defects due to human finitude "for which no one can be held morally responsible," and of the peculiar complexities of the present age. But this is no deterrent to the placing of a special emphasis on the view which detects "in the universe a destructive or demonic principle operating beyond the range of human volition." Stress is laid on "the Biblical [*sic*] view of the existence of a superhuman evil will or wills." There are "dark, irrational forces which surround and underlie human existence. Man is less secure in his control of things than former generations were disposed to believe. Human personality does not sit enthroned above the conflict directing its course, but may itself become the plaything of hidden powers."[2]

Modern psychology is again invoked in support of this view that "there are powerful, hidden, nameless forces on which human life is borne as on a tide and out of which consciousness arises, to illuminate, as some would say for a brief moment, like a flickering candle, the surrounding darkness. . . . The irrational, hidden forces which modern psychology has revealed in the individual life underlie the whole of human existence. To ignore these unfathom-

[1] 't Hooft and Oldham, *The Church and its Functions in Society*, p. 188.
[2] *Op. cit.*, p. 185.

able forces is to fail to understand the tragic nature of
human existence."[1] That the twists and complications
revealed by modern psychology bear no explanation other
than that of "an evil will that was set on defeating the
purpose of God" does not seem to be doubted. What is
fundamental in human life, it seems, is the "conflict
with superhuman forces of evil"[2] against which we can
do nothing 'by our own strength.'

An even gloomier view and a more incautious depreca-
tion of human endeavour is found in popularizations of
these 'orthodox' doctrines. Presented in rhetorical and
often extravagant terms, these influence opinion in a
way that cannot but fill us with foreboding. Consider a
recent contribution to the Christian News-Letter Books,
Divine Judgment in Human History, by D. R. Davies. This
book contains the substance of an annual York Diocesan
Lecture, it is dedicated to the late Archbishop Temple
and is warmly commended in a Foreword by the Bishop
of Hull. In substance, the book is an invitation to a
vilification of ourselves the very heartiness of which must
render it suspect. It is maintained that the attempt of
man to improve himself and his social environment is
itself the surest means of his downfall. The course of
history, compressed, as is the fashion in so many quarters,
with great facility into a rigid dialectical scheme, is
thought to have as its purpose to teach mankind "that
history itself is an impossible experiment."[3] As the matter
is also elegantly put, "history (i.e. trying to live in defiance
of God's will) is a mug's game."[4] "Whatever originates
from the will of man remains self-destructive."[5] "But in
the ruins of each illusion, man, with an optimistic
determination worthy of a better cause, rises to a fresh

---

[1] *Op. cit.*, p. 187.   [2] *Op. cit.*, p. 187.
[3] *Divine Judgment in Human History*, p. 19.
[4] *Op. cit.*, p. 20.   [5] *Op. cit.*, p. 19.

illusion, which, in our day, happens to be Socialism of some kind or another. Socialism, if it is ever tried, will be no more successful than its historic predecessors in overcoming the basic contradiction of human nature. Nothing human can ever do that. But let man try. That is why God has made man free. He will discover it won't work."[1] The civilizations of the past must all be viewed in this way as lessons in the futility of human effort. "They run the gamut of origin, rise, development and decay, all of which constitute a single process in successive phases. It is a process in which inherent contradiction matures to final destruction."[2] And in the more recent examples the process comes to its climax with greater rapidity. For "God is becoming impatient. The Holy Ghost is in a hurry."[3]

That crudities of this sort, so utterly lacking in historical or philosophical analysis, should have won for the writer a high place in the esteem of religious leaders and, as I understand, a large following among humbler ranks, is a sobering thought. It should give us pause before we assume that the theories which isolate religion from life will be slow to ally themselves effectively with the forces of reaction in the more democratic and liberal countries.

Most conspicuously absent from the despondent views we have noted, and the gloomy view of man's ethical possibilities on which they are based, is fair consideration of the complicated character of modern civilization. It is easy to say, and it is in fact often said from the pulpit and on the public platform, that man's inventiveness and his material skill have developed out of proportion to his ability to control his powers and direct the resources he can command to-day to suitable ends. Ethical progress, it is said, lags far behind scientific progress and general intellectual advance. Man has become exceedingly clever

[1] *Op. cit.*, p. 19. [2] *Op. cit.*, p. 18. [3] *Op. cit.*, p. 20.

but he is still very wicked. This is one of those popular clichés which have much superficial plausibility but will not bear careful scrutiny. For it takes little account of the fact that those scientific discoveries which have enhanced so considerably man's control over nature have also flung new and bewildering problems in his path. We have to remember especially the growing inter-dependence of our affairs in the social and economic sphere, both within a particular State and in the relations of States to one another. The world is rapidly dwindling, and the repercussions of one event are swiftly felt in parts remote from it. There lies before us therefore to-day the formidable task of organizing a new civilization, and a complicated industrial one, on the most comprehensive scale the world has ever known. Whether conditions are ripe for some 'world court' or a similar political institution to regulate men's relationships everywhere is another matter. But that is the goal we must eventually reach if disorders, sudden privations and conflicts are to be avoided; and the end must be achieved with as little prejudice as possible to those cultural varieties by which civilization is deepened and enriched. Nor must compre-hensive planning be allowed to jeopardize the freedom of the individual. The task is moreover complicated by the problem of backward races to whom the technological advances of modern civilization become available at a rate too rapid to allow the habits and institutions of civilized life to take a deep root in their character. That a scientific civilization tends inevitably to extend its range to all corners of the world does indeed substantially heighten the prospects of eventual stability. It mitigates, and may eventually remove, one of the most serious factors in the downfall of earlier civilizations—a hostile barbaric power beyond their borders. But in the mean-time the problems of a period of transition are sharply accentuated. There is no reason to believe that they cannot be surmounted eventually. Scientific advances make the prospects far brighter *on the whole*. But it is not to be wondered at that there should also be serious breakdowns, that relatively trivial happenings should be able to throw great organizations out of gear, that there should be anomalies such as the withholding of food from the hungry and its notorious destruction to keep up the prices, that unemployment, financial and economic crises, gross inequalities in the distribution of material goods, to mention only a few outstanding matters, should make life precarious and lustreless for multitudes of men even in the more fortunate and prosperous countries. Neither is it surprising that misfortunes of this kind should be the cause of much bitterness, that issues should be seen more sharply than is warranted in black and white, that men should suspect malice or jealousy where there is only stupidity or the sheer force of circumstances. Misrepresentations of this sort are quite understandable human failings. We must not, it is true, be so benign or 'innocent' as to disregard the presence of deliberate selfishness and evil design. But there is no special reason for assuming that it is on the increase. The contrary seems to me assuredly true. When therefore we have due regard to such considerations as we have advanced in this passage, it seems plain that we need not postulate 'satanic forces,' or represent the life of man as the working out of the tragic consequences of his utter wickedness, in order to account for the calamities and conflicts by which the foundations of society are shaken to-day.

To disentangle all the factors that contribute to social ills is a difficult task, and there would be perhaps little agreement about their relative force. But, fortunately, we have not to embark on any such enquiry here. It will suffice to indicate the sort of confusions upon which despondent views of man's ethical attainment thrive. When these are dispelled, and but little reflection is needed for the purpose, we can turn to our constructive tasks fortified by sober considerations such as that which Professor H. J. Paton presents in the following observation:

"The world may in many ways be ill-organized but the spectacle of modern civilization, with its infinitely varied activities all fitting in, to a certain extent, although no one really apprehends or wills the whole in detail, is one which would, I imagine, fill an inexperienced but intelligent observer from another planet with a considerable measure of respect."[1]

This brings us to a matter that we need to emphasize especially.

In regard to great social ills the individual can only be effective in close co-operation with others. When, as in times of war or economic distress, the world becomes a wilderness (but less so as we have seen than might appear at first), this is not because a number of independent individuals are simultaneously idle in the cultivation of their particular plots. Social action is concerted action, more so than ever to-day. And the new Jerusalem must be built up, not, as in the Biblical story, by each building before his own house, but by organized corporate action. This, as we have seen, induces the belief that responsibility is social, that men must be praised or condemned *en bloc*. But the true conclusion, as we also saw, is that more of our failures than we realize are not to be imputed, in the strict moral sense, to anyone. The failure of joint undertakings on a large scale is usually more indicative of failure, through finite limitations, to combine individual efforts effectively than of evil intention. Ills that arise from defects in the structure of society are no strict measure of the merit or demerit of

[1] *The Good Will*, p. 265.

its members. To ascertain the latter we have to ask what each individual could have done to avert those ills. And we shall find in a great many cases that very little was in fact possible. We might have been more politically minded in the inter-war period, we might have pressed more eagerly for reforms, but, given the situation as it was then, and having regard especially to the absence of any clear leadership, can we really suppose that there was a great deal more for ordinary men and women to do than they did? I suspect, in fact, that the older generation, in an excess of sensitivity at the outbreak of a second world war within the lifetime of its members, is somewhat too prone to reproach itself for its behaviour in a most uncertain and swiftly changing situation. We declare, again, very confidently that the German people ought to have foreseen and prevented the rise of Hitler. That there was little they could do in a short time once the Nazi régime was established the more sympathetic will readily allow, although some very hard things have been said on this matter also. But, it will be urged, there was ample opportunity earlier. But was there? Who precisely should have seized this opportunity? Whom exactly could we reproach? Notorious leaders certainly. Such delusions as they suffered will hardly extenuate the brutalities they deliberately initiated. But what shall we say of the ordinary German? Given the situation, its bewilderment and convulsions and privations, how much can we seriously expect him to have foreseen, how exactly do we suggest that each individual, in his station, should have set about averting disaster? To put the matter otherwise, what proportion of Germans willed the evils in which their nation was subsequently engulfed, even in the more negative way of passive aquiescence? Some deliberate evil and witting indifference there must have been, and it would be an ill service to Germany and to the world to whitewash them. As we have also noted, even where there is no malicious intent the remedy may still be severe. But when we 'sit down in a cool hour' are we not bound to conclude that the German people as a whole, on the whole, have been more sinned against than sinning? Taking thus as our test the question what each individual did and could have done, and bearing in mind the discussion and persuasion normally required to initiate reform, we shall find, I think, that the complicated character of modern society, not merely sets before us exceptionally difficult problems, but, also, sets severe limits on the efficacy of the individual when he does discern the remedy. This must be constantly remembered when pessimism is so ready to feed itself gluttonously on the vilification of man.

Present society does indeed enable certain individuals, in positions of power or authority, to bring about an exceptional amount of good or bad, as they choose, although it may be doubted whether the delicacy of the social mechanism makes this possible in a greater degree than did the obtuseness of the masses under the great despotisms of the past. For this the remedy clearly lies in close democratic control. The development of a better democracy, affording greater scope for consultation and discussion, will also minimize the impotence of the individual. To that extent the fortunes of a community and the ways it follows will be a better picture of its ethical attainment. But at present they afford a most imperfect insight into properly moral qualities.

CHAPTER X

COMPROMISE AND MORAL EVIL

THE LIMITATIONS ON INDIVIDUAL conduct which arise from the necessity of acting as a member of society, and not in some isolated sphere of one's own, have induced some thinkers to conclude that we are altogether restricted to the 'duties of our station' as prescribed by society. That, as I have urged, is an entirely unwarranted deduction, but it is also one that has played a not unimportant part in the spread of pessimistic views. The true account of the matter, as was stressed early in this essay, is that there is an ultimate right and wrong to every situation, and in terms of this it is possible for an individual to disagree with the view of his society as to where his duty lies. When he does so, or when he considers others to be mistaken about the course of their duties, it is incumbent upon him to use all available means to correct the notions which he considers mistaken and to press for such alterations and reforms as will bring the practice of his society more into conformity with the standards that commend themselves to him. By infusing a spirit of self-lessness and consideration into his own conduct he will also help to raise the general standard of behaviour and clarify the ideals of his fellows. All this, of course, must be undertaken with restraint and humility. A sense of our own fallibility as well as that of our society should accompany the effort to instruct others. Regard should be had to the experience that has gone to the framing of social standards, and we should be particularly cautious in pronouncing on matters which extend beyond the range of our own experience. In some respects, indeed, it is well to defer to the opinions of those who are better informed, or better placed to judge, than we are ourselves, even in respect to actions that we must perform ourselves. And when it comes, as it may on some important issue, to the question of actually disobeying the laws of the State, and proceeding in an unconstitutional manner, we have both to make the fullest allowance for our own fallibility and to weigh very carefully the considerable ills that attend upon a break in law-abiding habits and orderly procedure against such advantages to society or such a fulfilment of moral claims as we expect to accrue from the resistance to what we consider an unrighteous demand. Resistance, especially in democratic countries, is only to be justified in highly exceptional circumstances. Whether it is justified in some respect or other must be decided in the last resort by the individual himself, and if he himself is assured that the course he is following is the one obligatory upon him, he is free from blame even when he is in fact mistaken. On that score enough was said earlier. The point to be stressed at the moment is that a person who understands aright the relation in which he stands to his neighbour, and to the order of society, will perceive also the necessity of adapting his own conduct to that of others even when this is not prompted by ethical principles—a necessity which will clearly be greater in public than in more private matters but which is hardly absent from any sphere of human conduct because there is hardly any respect in which our conduct does not require some co-operation from others. Departure from the ideals that commend themselves to us may thus be required in the interest of the greatest fulfilment on the whole of moral requirements.

Compromises of this nature have always lain heavily on the minds of sincere and devoted Christians. In the early days of the Christian Church there were factors which prevented the issue from becoming acute. For not only was it thought that 'the last things' were really imminent, but the Christian community was small in number and conditions of life fairly simple. It was possible to approximate fairly closely to the ideals in which that community itself believed. But it could not continue so for long. And with the spread of the Christian Church the problem of its involvement in a pagan society became very acute. Should the Church endeavour to maintain itself as a self-subsistent society acknowledging no allegiance other than to Christ and living as strictly as possible by Christian standards? This alternative had manifold attractions, but it became altogether impossible for a Church that had established itself in all parts of the Roman Empire. Individuals or brotherhoods might live in relative isolation, and they could, by the earnestness of their devotion, help to hold up the Christian ideal before society in general—although the strain which they put on themselves sometimes resulted in entirely opposite effects. But whatever purpose, either by way of witnessing to special principles, or by performance of special acts of worship to God, compensated for this withdrawal from the world on the part of particular individuals, Christians in general had to maintain themselves as members of societies where the Christian ideal was only partly acknowledged and most imperfectly understood. They had thus to come to terms with practices and ideals inferior to their own and follow a 'relative' law distinct from the 'absolute' law of Christ, a distinction which received so celebrated a formulation by St. Augustine at a very critical moment in the history of the Christian Church. This, for the most part, has been the procedure of Christians throughout the centuries, sometimes more, sometimes less, clearly articulated. It has not indeed, at any time won universal acceptance. There have always been Christians opposed to any compromise with the world, and they have in many cases helped to deepen the awareness of Christian responsibilities. For compromise is fraught with the very greatest dangers and it is altogether essential for the Church to remain uneasy about a lowering of its standards even when required by the most unavoidable circumstances. Christians have been far too prone to acquiesce in accepted practices instead of straining after the fullest attainment of Christian ideals possible in the world at a particular time. The Church has even lent its cloak to undisputably wicked practices. Setting itself up as the trustee of the conscience of society it has allowed society to drift in many a stormy sea with very little guidance from conscience. The fanatic and the impractical idealist are therefore not without their function, but it is a limited one, and one which again we should be careful not to exploit. For the fanatic can hardly be effective unless he has every assurance himself of the soundness of his views—a matter overlooked, I believe, by some pacifists who consider that they can help society by adhering to principles which they themselves believe to be impracticable for society generally. And however much we may be tempted to allow for the usefulness of blind adherents to a limited principle, or a principle not immediately practicable,[1] it is quite plain that society cannot be generally composed of enthusiasts of that sort. The policy of isolation from society, is, moreover, less practicable to-day than at any time past. Our habits make us more dependent on existing economic systems, there is no New World for which we can set our sails, there is hardly a desert where the glare of publicity will not

---

[1] Whether pacifism is a practicable course is another matter on which no opinion need be offered here.

find us out. If we are to be hermits it can only be by making a cell for ourselves within a social organization and with a hearty measure of endorsement of its ways even when we are most squeamish about soiling ourselves with them. Moreover, there remains the express petition of Christ on behalf of his followers that they should remain *in* the world even if they were not wholly *of* it. And to be in the world is to come to terms with much that is evil and imperfect in it.

No one who has not felt in his inmost soul the agony of coming to terms with evil, who has not struggled to find his way through an entanglement of ethical problems, who has not found himself at variance with friends and the advocates of the same creed as himself, has come to ethical maturity. Even privations and martyrdom do not fully ensure this. We fall short of the full stature of a moral personality if we depend on simplifications of problems which present all manner of complications to a sensitive conscience. Compromise, and the struggle not to compromise more than we need or to find in the exigencies of a difficult situation excuses for suiting our own convenience, prescribe for us a very essential part of the 'fellowship of His sufferings.'

What follows? Not, and this is the point to which the present discussion leads, that any person who lowers his standard, or departs from ideals upon which he thinks society ought to organize itself, can be held in any way disloyal to his principles if the departure seems to him most expedient on the whole in view of a failure of others to accept these principles or their reluctance to follow them. It is not essentially a sin to compromise. On the contrary it may express considerable saintliness. But so much has compromise in the present legitimate sense been confused with compromise in the bad sense, namely a concession to our own weakness, that the departure of Christians from the standards they profess has come to be regarded as inherently sinful. Indeed, in some quarters it is presented, without further analysis as supreme sinfulness, a betrayal of principles we have ourselves accepted, a sin against the light and revelation which we ourselves acclaim. It is so if, as was noted, it is a concession to weakness, although we should remember here also that the severity of a temptation mitigates the blame. But departure from Christian standards is far from being altogether of this kind. And the complaint which can, I think, be very fairly made against the gloomy theological views so prevalent to-day, is that they fail to draw the distinction we have just noted between the two meanings of compromise, and inveigh with the force of all the rhetoric they can command against present society as a whole for failures which a great many of its members deplore, and which they would certainly avoid were the matter entirely in their hands.

Very closely related to the failure to exonerate members of society sufficiently for departures from principle which are forced upon them by circumstances they cannot control, is the arraignment of men for limitations in their ethical judgments due to the ways in which they are affected by their community in the formation of such judgments. Niebuhr is especially fond of stressing the extent to which we are immersed in this way in the 'relativities of history.' But here again the limitation to which we are subject is not one for which we can justly be held responsible provided we have done all we can to rid ourselves of such prejudices as society tends to perpetuate and harden.

Many of the confusions traceable to these sources could moreover be dispelled more easily were they properly separated from one another. When Niebuhr, for example, speaks of 'the relativities of history,' it is

E

never quite plain whether he is thinking of compromises forced upon us by society, of conditions made inevitable by limitations of finite existence itself and thus not removable under any conditions we know, of mistaken judgments due to the age and society in which we live, or of the perversion of conduct due to selfishness by which, in his view, all human conduct is affected. Were the author's views in these respects set out in more systematic fashion we would be in a much better position to determine their soundness.

A word may be added here about the notion of an 'impossible ideal' which has figured largely in recent Neo-Protestant theology and to which Niebuhr, to refer to him again, attaches especial importance. An ideal may be said to be impossible in the sense that it refers to conditions which can be brought about in the future if we discharge our obligations now. But since there is some relation of this nature between most of our future duties and our duties here and now, there does not seem to be anything in particular to be gained by referring to future duties as impossible ideals. It will be a better expedient to urge one another to take as comprehensive a view as may be of the range of our duties and shape our course at the present in the light of what will be eventually of most value for society as a whole. But we shall have to remember carefully that in so far as our conduct at some particular time closes avenues of useful service at a later date, it is for the measure in which we deliberately incurred this limitation, and not for the subsequent failure, that we are morally accountable. An ideal may, again, be impossible, in the sense that we are ignorant of its nature. That there are ideals which are made impossible for us in this way is not unimportant. For it sets before us the aim of making our consciences as enlightened as we can. It is a reminder of our fallibility.

But 'outer' or 'objective' duty is a better designation here, for it will help us to remember that failure which is due to inability to discern the real nature of a duty is not blameworthy in the strict moral sense. Finally, it may be useful to abstract from the full conditions of the situations in which we have to act and consider what would be desirable 'under more ideal conditions.' Many utopias have been built in this way, many 'patterns set up in heaven' exposed to our sight. And these have a highly useful purpose to serve. For even where the limitations can never be fully removed, a simplified picture may help us to centre our attention on essentials and discriminate more effectively between the ends which are in fact open to us in actual and immediate situations. To flirt with the impossible in the present sense will extend our ethical horizon and will rid us of narrow prejudices, it will allow imagination to have its proper place in the moral life, it will enable the 'dreamers of dreams' to become more effectively the 'movers and shakers of the world.' But, notwithstanding all such advantages, the utmost caution must be exercised if the notion of an impossible ideal is not to mislead us seriously. For it can never be the standard by which moral guilt and merit are determined. These depend, not on what would be possible under special conditions, nor on what may become possible eventually, not even on what we could see to be possible here and now if our judgment and our moral imagination were sharper, but *solely on the individual's loyalty to the ideal that presents itself to him*. And it is because of its proneness to obscure this elementary ethical truth that the term 'impossible ideal' should be used very cautiously—if at all.

In this connection we are reminded also of the proneness to equate the opposition of interests which characterizes finite life at every stage with overt conflict of selfish wills.

Outstanding ethical and social thinkers in recent centuries have tended to write as though the genuine good of one person could never be opposed to the 'true' good of another. And they have held it to be their business especially to sustain the position and justify altruism in a most Gilbertian fashion by showing that when we serve the community we are also in fact promoting our own best interest. This strain can be traced from the undisguised individualism of the seventeenth century, through Rousseau's celebrated and most paradoxical notion of the 'general will' and the common good, to the great idealist thinkers of the last century. It becomes most articulate in Green's insistence that 'the True Good' is not competitive,[1] and in some ways it affords the most important clue to the course of social and political thought in the modern period.[2] But it is clearly very ill conceived, for we are throughout our lives choosing between incompatible goods. The conflicts and perplexities by which we are most sharply awakened from moral complacency, and which present us with some of our most agonizing, if also ennobling, experiences, have their origin in this limitation of finite life. This is one of the most important ways in which the world is a 'vale of soul-making.' Both in our more private concerns and in our public conduct we have thus constantly to be selecting between incompatible goods. And the anxiety to obscure this most essential feature of finite existence seems to be mainly due to a reluctance to admit that altruistic action is possible. It has been thought necessary, in one ingenious way or another, to commend their duties to men by assuring them that they invariably stand to gain by discharging a duty. Niebuhr, entering very largely into this cynical view, a

[1] *Prolegomena to Ethics*, Book III, Chapter 4.

[2] As I have tried to show in my forthcoming *The Individualism of T. H. Green.*

view which in fact precludes morality, has little difficulty in showing, in his recent *The Children of Light and the Children of Darkness*, that the attempt to reconcile our interests at every point breaks down entirely. But, instead of being content merely to insist that moral theory does not require us to strain ingenuity to the limit in an attempt at the reconciliation of all genuine goods, he opposes to the assumption which he criticizes the view that there is some element of malicious conflict in every human relationship. The failure to distinguish clearly between incompatibility of interest and overt conflict is not the sole reason for Niebuhr's conclusion. But if the distinction were sharply drawn, as he does not draw it, it would be less easy for him, and others, to form such distorted pictures of man's ethical attainment.

This, then, is the sum of the matter. By forming our view of the morality of human conduct, not on the basis of such loyalty to the agent's own ideal as our experience warrants us to attribute to men, but in terms of their conformity collectively, in substance as well as intention, to the pattern of an ideal society or of the Kingdom of God, we exaggerate the extent of sinful action. Thereby we set in the path of progress obstacles of our own making, we obtrude into a situation already sufficiently complicated and fraught with dangers, complications that have no foundation outside our own misconceptions and heated imagination. The most immediate result is a substantial reduction of our estimate of the progress and reform which is possible for society. Some reaction against a facile optimism which took little account of considerable difficulties rooted in the complexities of man's nature and the structure of society was indeed due. Belief in inevitable progress, in the automatic adjustment of conflict, in the mysterious providence of 'the hidden hand,' could not but lead to an apathetic surrender to the drift of events. But the real cure for this situation is a proper understanding of the nature of the evils that beset us, and especially of the precise part played in them by deliberate moral evil. Unless that understanding is achieved we shall continue to set in the path of our own actions, and those of society generally, the bogey of great evils for which there is no foundation in fact.

CHAPTER XI

THE LIBERAL ALTERNATIVE

THE PRINCIPLES ON WHICH we have proceeded in this essay, and the emphasis placed on personal responsibility, bring us into very close accord with the main trend of liberal theology. Liberalism stresses especially the worth and freedom of the individual. But not every liberal theologian sees the issue plainly, and of late there have been some serious misunderstandings about the implications of a liberal view. Before giving some indication of their nature, very briefly as it does not come strictly within our purpose, I should like to refer to a book which should, in my view, be kept very much to the fore in all discussions of morals and theology.

This is *The Concept of Sin*, by F. R. Tennant. This book takes its stand on the view that sin is morally imputable action. As the author puts it, the Christian doctrine of sin is particularly incompatible with the ascription of sinfulness to "activities to which ethics refuses the category of moral accountability."[1] The evidence adduced from the Scriptures themselves in support of this principle is all the more telling because of the prevalent assumption that it is just the faithful adherence to the message of the Bible itself, in the New Testament as well as the Old, which requires a departure from the 'common-sense' view of the nature of sin. It is also shown that the conditions of accountability, as they present themselves normally to the moral consciousness, receive unique confirmation and emphasis in the teaching of Jesus—contrary to much that is carelessly thought at the present time.

[1] *Op cit.*, p. 34.

In describing the conditions of responsibility and guilt Tennant stresses the fact that "there is more than one specific kind of value."[1] He goes very carefully into the distinction between 'merit' and 'virtue' or 'perfection,' this being his way of presenting what is more commonly described nowadays by the terms 'moral' and 'non-moral' value. Perfection depends on natural endowment and nurture. It consists largely in the "active imagination required for the fullest exercise of sympathy and considerateness, the impulsiveness which can lend unique grace to kindness and courtesy, the ready tact which can discover the right word or devise the right action at the moment."[2] "Such gifts and graces" are "for the most part quite beyond the ability of the will to create or to command."[3] But merit must be won. It is "proportionate to the intensity of the struggle," and not, in any measure, to the soundness of our judgment or to some quality of the content at which we aim. In many cases we find that "where virtue increases, merit *must* decrease; for the more reluctance is overcome, the less remains to be coerced."[4] This has to be admitted if we are not to belie that freedom of choice whereby it can be quite unambiguously stated that the sinner "could perfectly well have acted differently"; and without which "we could not reproach, though we might compassionate ourselves or our neighbours for 'choosing' the worse course."[5] The self must then be regarded as "character plus something more"; " 'in the something more than character' which the moral self includes—in its transcendence and partial independence of all past experience—lies the real spring of moral decision."[6] Following these principles the doctrine of sin can be summarized in these terms.

"If sin be activity for which the agent is responsible,

[1] *Op. cit.*, p. 63. [2] *Op. cit.*, p. 62. [3] *Op. cit.*, p. 62.
[4] *Op. cit.*, p. 56. [5] *Op. cit.*, p. 171. [6] *Op. cit.*, p. 166.

accountable, and guilty; and if, conversely, no human activity for which the agent is irresponsible and unaccountable, and which, consequently, cannot be regarded by God as guilty, is ever capable of being rightly called sinful: then, it has been maintained, a sin must always possess the following four characteristics. Firstly, it must be a violation of a moral law, an aberration from an ethical standard or ideal. Secondly, the law of which a given act, capable of being imputed as sin, is an outward or objective transgression, must be known, or be capable of being known, and known as binding upon himself, by the agent. Thirdly, until virtue be won, there must be two lines of conduct open to the actor, to each of which he is impelled by impulses of different intensity and moral value. And lastly, the activity must be the outcome of intention, and of choice characterized by the freedom which the subject's will possesses."[1]

The implications of these principles are examined very carefully by Tennant and set out in clear, unmistakable terms. He pays close attention to such misunderstandings as arise from failure to draw fundamental distinctions. Outwardly the account of such distinctions is a little dated. Moral philosophers to-day would give a more satisfactory account of the distinction between the 'psychical' and 'psychological' standpoints (Chapter VII) in terms of the notion of a 'subjective' and an 'objective' meaning of value. They would also, as we have observed, prefer to speak of non-moral value than of perfection. In describing the latter, Tennant also lays himself open to criticism from one important school of moral philosophers on account of the concessions he makes to idealism. But these are not important matters here, and it has to be remembered that *The Concept of Sin* appeared[2] before the close analytical thinking about ethical principles initiated

[1] *Op. cit.*, p. 209. [2] In 1912.

by such thinkers as G. E. Moore and H. A. Prichard had made itself felt. All that matters for us now is that here we have a straightforward presentation of such conditions of guilt and responsibility as would, in all essentials, commend themselves to any enlightened ethical consciousness, together with an indication of the emphasis and enrichment these conditions receive in the teaching of Jesus. If the representatives of the New Protestantism choose to set aside such matters altogether and repudiate in effect, if not always in name, the ideas of freedom and individual responsibility, then we are certainly entitled to a clear indication of the *precise* points at which such seemingly incontrovertible principles as those put forward by Tennant, are mistaken. This is not forthcoming. Instead we have vague denunciations and a bland, one might even say arrogant, refusal to consider the position. But this will not do at all. The matter lies right at the heart of the struggle of our civilization for very existence, and we can ill afford to waste our substance in the fantastic tussles of a grotesque theological tournament, clad from head to toe in our own technicalities. Let the real challenge be taken up, let the real issue be joined. If Tennant and other liberal thinkers are mistaken, then let us be told *just where* they are mistaken. To dismiss their books with contempt as 'Pelagian treatises' is sheer evasion. For what if Pelagius after all were more right than his detractors?

The insistence on a need for a fair confrontation of the liberal claim must not be allowed to obscure for us the difficulties of the problem of freedom upon which the controversy must ultimately centre. The most that we have ventured to plead for in this essay is the recognition of the principle that moral responsibility belongs entirely to the individual and depends, not upon outward conduct, but upon loyalty to one's own ideal. So much seems elementary and beyond dispute. But when we consider more closely how such 'loyalty' is to be conceived we are immediately faced with difficulties that are apt to dishearten all but the stoutest thinkers. On the one hand, in the actual moment of acting there seems to be an immediate assurance of freedom—as has often been pointed out. On the other hand, it is exceptionally hard to represent to ourselves the possibility of acting in such wise that our choice is not determined for us in some way or another. But this is none the less the problem to which we must address ourselves. That it is an 'age-long' problem around which controversy has raged almost more than any other, far from being a sound reason for shelving it to-day, only serves to accentuate its importance and centrality. The assumption, peculiarly prevalent among philosophers in recent years and not uncommon in theology, that we can turn our minds to other matters where more substantial results can be expected, shows a most insidious confusion in our thought. For the problem of freedom is most intimately connected with the problems of 'the right and the good,' of motive and intention, to which philosophers have turned with such eagerness of late. Any theory that we advance about these topics presupposes some view or other about free om, and there seems to be no more certain or more important lesson to be learnt from the course of ethical studies in the past thirty years than the futility of seeking to isolate the problem of freedom or defer discussion of it un il other matters are settled. It is a problem to be faced at the start and kept to the fore throughout the treatment of most other ethical questions. The proper benefit of the advances recently made in ethics, and their contribution to cognate studies, cannot be felt until this lesson is well and truly learnt. But the problem of freedom is, also, not one to be touched upon briefly in drawing to a close. And to the general insistence that this is the problem above all others whose challenge must be boldly taken up, and one which we can only disregard at the peril of such despair and atrophy as will inevitably follow the maddening attempt to piece together the parts of a puzzle without some essential clues, to this I wish only to add two comments which can, I think, be made without transgressing the limits we have assigned to ourselves in this essay.

The first is that in some regards there has been a better understanding of the nature of the problem of moral freedom than at any time past, and, in consequence, the removal of some difficulties that had seemed very formidable and crucial. Of these the following is the most important. It used to be thought that the notion of absolute freedom of choice implied the possibility that any action could be expected from any person at any time. Such a consequence would clearly be disastrous to any theory. It would make worse than lunatics of us and not responsible agents, and it would be contrary to all experience. But freedom of choice is clearly not required by ethical theory except within the limits of such conflict as there may be between duty and interest. When our characters, as formed at a certain stage in our history, draw us in a direction contrary to the one required by duty or by our conscience, then, and then only, is our action properly unpredictable and free in the libertarian sense. Nothing in my character induces me at the moment to hurl myself into the fire, and I can think of nothing in the present circumstances which could persuade me that it is a duty to do so. There can therefore be no possibility of my acting in such fashion. There is thus no moral conflict, nor any issue of a properly ethical character, in my abstention from such folly. But if my friend falls into the fire, and I am too cowardly by nature and training to risk injury by putting out the flames that envelop him, then there arises the question, can I, other things being as they are, make a free effort of will to succour my friend in spite of my natural disinclination; can we conceive an effort to do so which has not its springs somewhere in my nature. I do not propose to tackle the question. What I do wish to stress is simply that the question whether or not there are free efforts of will must be confined to the cases where there is a conflict between character and duty, and where there is, therefore, nothing to militate against the normal continuity and reasonableness of conduct. To this extent the libertarians have, I think, clearly and convincingly answered their critics,[1] and the more plainly this is understood the better placed will we be generally for intelligent consideration of all questions which touch upon the problem of choice. As to whether choice within the limits described can be fairly distinguished from blind chance and regarded as behaviour for which we are morally accountable, as to whether its being thought of as a conscious effort (or refusal to make one) makes it really credible, I do not care at the moment to enquire. But there is a further matter in connection with such choices which I wish to stress.

It is only for a certain type of ethical theory that freedom of choice is essential. This is the type that retains the ideas of ultimate obligation, guilt, and praise or blame. If, therefore, it proves impossible to show that there is genuine freedom of choice or to conceive of the latter in a way compatible with the requirements of responsibility, it will still be possible to draw important distinctions of value between different kinds of conduct. The price we pay for repudiating the idea of freedom will

[1] Cf. *Scepticism and Construction*, by C. A. Campbell, Chapter V.

indeed be a high one, and it will lead to a very general impoverishment in the life of man. But it does not follow that all will be lost. The alternative will not be material- ism or hedonism or some other crude form of naturalism. For certain qualities of mind and character have supreme inherent worth which is not directly affected by the value exhibited in free "conscientious willing." Ethics, on the present view, will be mainly concerned with these. And it should be emphasized here that there has been very notable ethical thinking which confined itself to the sphere of such quasi-æsthetic values. Such for the most part was the course followed by Greek ethical thought. The idea of 'obligation' did not present itself sharply to the Greeks and they were never very acutely conscious of the problem of freedom. The problem of the good life would be mainly for them how may the true well being of the agent himself be achieved, in what environment and by what training is a man to reach that state of himself, or to acquire that character, in which his own nature is fulfilled. It was thus possible for Aristotle to take over from the study of biology the conceptions which were fundamental in his attempt to understand the good life. Conceived in this way, morality would be primarily a matter of right thinking; as the celebrated Socratic maxim put it, virtue was knowledge. So far as there was a problem of freedom, it arose, not from a postulate of the moral life itself, but from the sheer fact that in actual practice men seem to choose the worse knowing the better. Plato and Aristotle exerted themselves to deal with this problem, contending in their several ways that knowledge of the 'better' could not be *real* knowledge in such cases, but only opinion or, as in the case of Aristotle, 'latent' knowledge. The good was akin to what was deepest and most essential in man, and when fairly perceived it attracted him more than anything else. According to

Aristotle the good is the fulfilment of our own latent tendencies. It requires freedom, but only in the sense in which the artist must be free or the sense in which the best qualities of the mind are to be educed by free rather than mechanical training. And this is altogether different from the problem of freedom which confronts us when the idea of obligation, derived largely from the Hebrews and deepened by Christian teaching, becomes central to ethical thinking proper. It does not follow, of course, that the study of conditions by which the best qualities of mind and character are attained has little place in ethical theory. But they will not come into our account of strictly *moral* value. The problem of freedom here will be the problem of the unique choice presupposed by guilt, remorse, and blame, as these ideas appear in an ultimate moral reference. It is, I think, of the very utmost importance to keep apart the two conceptions of freedom and the types of value which require them. Failure to do so is responsible for a great deal of confusion in the ethical thought of the last three hundred years. And it seems to me also very necessary at the moment to go very carefully into the question what sort of picture of the good life we can form if we boldly leave out the notion of responsibility and guilt. We shall thus have alternative views much more fairly presented to us. The alternative just mentioned—namely, the one which does not presuppose ultimate choice and responsibility—accords *in some ways* much more easily than the first with essential features of religious life, and especially with the doctrine of 'grace.' In our attempt to understand it and relate it to the religious life as a whole, we shall, moreover, learn a great deal from the kind of theologian whom we have ventured to criticize somewhat harshly in this volume. For, as I observed above in discussing the views of Brunner, what they do in fact is to put forward an essentially Socratic view of the good life into which there have been imported quite incompatible ideas of guilt and responsibility—Brunner himself, as we noted, is quite severe in his strictures on the ethics of duty with 'autonomy' as its requirement. But while we can pay tribute on this score to the traditionalists, and acknowledge an immense debt to them for our understanding of the nature of one of the two main alternatives between which we must choose in framing our final view of the relations between ethics and religion, we must not be tempted for a moment to underestimate the serious nature of the confusion which infects their thought when they retain, within the framework of an ultimate determinism, the ideas of guilt and accountability. If the ethic of duty goes by the board, the notion of guilt must go also, and with it praise and blame in an ultimate ethical sense. That would be a very serious business for Christian theology, and the present writer is far from being convinced that such a sacrifice of our worth and dignity has to be made. But the most that is stressed in this paragraph is the need to confront the issues fairly. If it does prove that a sacrifice of something that had seemed essential has to be made, then let us be bold about it and cut ourselves loose from entanglement with the wreckage of cherished and time-honoured illusions.

It should be added that the need for a close co-operation between the moral philosopher and the theologian seems particularly evident in regard to the matters touched upon in the preceding passage.

The failure of traditionalist theology to give an account of sin and moral evil which can be reconciled with the demands of the moral consciousness, together with insistence on the inexpungeable character of our ultimate ethical convictions, has been the main theme of this book. And while, as has just been indicated, the view which conceives of the evil in men's lives in terms other than sinfulness in the proper meaning deserves serious consideration, it is just not possible to retain the idea of genuine sinfulness and guilt within the presuppositions of traditionalist theology. But prevarication is by no means confined to the traditionalists. Others, within the liberal fold, have sometimes shown themselves much disposed 'to have it both ways.'

At this point, especially as the present discussion is drawing to a close, the opportunity must be taken to pay some tribute to the Continental theologians on whom we have ventured to make the most severe strictures. They have the advantage of many liberal thinkers in two ways.

First of all, they have been unshaken in their conviction that human beings are guilty. Through paradox and sheer contradiction, and in the face of the most persistent criticism, they have resolutely stuck to their conviction that man is the bearer of supreme responsibility. And if, as seems to me certainly the case, we are in fact free and responsible agents, to keep before us the idea of this moral responsibility and present to us its sombre as well as its elevating features, is, indeed, some compensation for the blunting of the moral consciousness by the presentation of doctrines which are altogether incompatible with belief in a free moral life.

Another item to be put to the credit side of the New Theology is the consistency with which its representatives have developed the implications of the traditionalist doctrine. It is the wholehearted way in which they have accepted this doctrine, their resolute determination not to shrink from any of its consequences, that makes their position so vulnerable. They have carried the argument to an extreme which provides its own refutation, they have ventured upon such extravagant paradoxes that their own friends are appalled. But in fact they are simply saying openly and loudly what others have asserted for a long time in less deliberate and terrifying tones. It does not seem possible to be a consistent traditionalist without eventually joining hands with Barth and Brunner and Niebuhr. They themselves have helped to make this plain, and tribute must be paid them on that account. But it must also be said that they have only prepared the more effectively, albeit unwittingly, for the final overthrow of traditionalist theology.

I say this with boldness, and what to some will appear effrontery, as one who has himself sought a long time for a middle way. There just is no middle way. Either guilt has to be incurred deliberately or it has not. Sin cannot be in part the choice of the individual, in part the result of the fall or the 'sin of man.' The alternatives are quite exclusive, and the defiant paradoxes of the New Theology simply underline the inherent contradiction of attempts to retain the idea of freedom within a deterministic scheme. There can be no 'partial determinism,'[1] although there can be various kinds of determinism, and although many factors may contribute to the situation within which a choice must be made. If, therefore, we speak of the 'sin' of man or of some wickedness which infects the human situation as a whole and which cannot be identified with a sum total of the avoidable sins of individuals, the break with liberalism must be complete; for such notions have no room for individual freedom in any meaning we normally give to those terms—as we have insisted especially in earlier contexts. But if, on the other hand, we are loth to surrender liberal principles, we must be equally uncompromising in rejecting ideas

[1] An idea on which N. P. Williams draws very heavily in his *The Ideas of the Fall and of Original Sin*. See specially Lectures VII, p. 446.

that are bound up with the traditionalist view. And, in many cases, the liberals have proved as reluctant as the traditionalists to face the issue unflinchingly.

The New Theology thus serves to throw into sharp relief two common faults of liberalism. The first is the proneness of liberal thinkers to avert their gaze from the stark reality of sin and to turn to sentimental pictures of very excusable human failings and errors. Their benevolence has been apt to draw them away altogether from the problem, an enfeeblement which liberal thought has exhibited in other regards as well. For the catholicity of their sympathies make its protagonists somewhat too undiscriminating. Acutely conscious of men's susceptibility to prejudice, they have allowed their charity to over-reach and defeat itself by suiting their views too easily to the beliefs and moods of a particular time. From being the pioneers of new thought, proceeding in the spirit of free and critical enquiry, they have thus degenerated into the slaves of passing fashion. This is mere conservatism in reverse, and it was erected in the last century into a general principle by the spread of a facile belief in inevitable and continuous progress. In this way the liberal becomes, in a scientific age, a very fervent worshipper at the shrine of science, and the extravagant pretentions of science in spheres where its methods have no application, and its findings no relevance, owe much to the uncritical support of liberal thinkers. Examples present themselves from many quarters, both in regard to the popular and the more specialized discussion of religious questions. I will only mention here the uncritical use of the idea of evolution in religious philosophy over the past century, and, in very recent years, the exaggerated estimate of the relevance of physics to religious truth. For we must not be tempted too far from our subject. Our problem is the ethical one. And here the too accommodating temper of the liberal has often induced him to make the most damaging concessions to naturalism. The result may be seen at the moment in the popular appeal of such books as *Science and Ethics*, by C. H. Waddington, and in the claims made, often with the active concurrence of theologians, on behalf of psycho-analysis as the ultimate clue to ethical questions.[1] Your liberal therefore needs to be kept very strictly on the leash lest his impetuousness should lead him to squander the choicest of his own treasures. The ideas of responsibility, merit, guilt, obligation and value, as unique ethical ideas, are never very safe in his hands. That he should often empty them of genuine significance is not indeed so inherently repellent as is the spectacle of theologians sadistically lashing themselves and others for crimes which no one in particular seems to have perpetrated. The liberal can be counted on to take a kindly view, but his kindness may be fatal, and when he interprets the moral life of man too completely in terms of heredity and environment and such failures and setbacks as men naturally encounter in the long struggle of evolution, he is apt to surrender the uniquely individual quality of moral endeavour to impersonal cosmic forces as completely as the more immediately theatrical trans-cendentalism with whose threat to the moral life we have been mainly concerned. The liberal may in his own way require his soul of man as effectively as any.

Misplaced generosity and a failure to understand when the essentials of a position are compromised, together with a general absence of precision, is also evidenced in the second, but no less common, fault of liberal theology, namely acquiescence in aspects of traditionalist doctrine which are quite incompatible with liberal principles.

[1] See *Man, Morals and Society* by J. C. Flugel.

Here again appeasement has an irresistible lure for the liberal, and he is apt to regard a somewhat modified type of traditionalism as offering the basis of a negotiated peace that will spare himself and his antagonist the humiliation of surrender. For this reason liberalism often becomes an assortment of the most ill-adjusted elements. This brings in its train a host of complications, the acutest of them arising from the presentation of the difference between the liberal and the traditionalist as a difference of degree or a difference of emphasis and interpretation as between the adherents to a common view. Both, it is thought, can accept the idea of a fall and the ensuing corruption of man. But it is possible to take too gloomy a view of the matter. As opposed to the extremist doctrine of total corruption we have the more moderate belief in partial corruption, the divine image in man being obscured but not obliterated, or the idea of a 'corruption through and through' which none the less allows us to consider the elements which are subject to this infection to retain a large measure of their natural worth. And no doubt it makes a great difference to our practical attitude how far we are prepared to go with our doctrine of human corruption. But if we allow the doctrine at all we have really lifted the problem of sin out of the realm where the normal requirements of ethics retain their significance and individual decisions are crucial. Freedom is no longer a postulate, and once we admit the notion of sinfulness which is not freely willed, there is little serious hindrance to our straining credibility further by ascribing to a sinful human nature the blame for other ills and privations by which the human situation as a whole is characterized. From this the descent into Barthianism is easy, and if we are held from it by the starkness and ruthlessness of its claims, our position will still be a most unenviable one on the shifting sands of uneasy compromises with no truth to which we can surely and firmly cling.

Some intimation of the troubles that await us here has been given above in discussing the views of Professor Quick. To pursue the matter into further detail now would take us far afield. But I should like to refer the reader to one example of liberalism drifting from its moorings to the undertow of a prevailing fashion. In a recent volume of studies in liberal theology there is one essay by J. C. Bennett in which the author tries to prepare for 'a fresh synthesis in Christian thinking about man' by exhibiting the "insights which many liberals have learned to accept under the tutelage of Augustinian theologians and of the harrowing experiences of our generation." [1] After stressing the idea of freedom and describing the belief in man as a creative responsible self as a "characteristic of liberalism which must not be lost," he comes, by way of tributes to Niebuhr and Brunner, to the following admission:

"Sin is disobedience to God which has its root in human freedom. Formerly, I believed that the use of the word must be limited to those choices which are made in full understanding that they are opposed to the will of God when we have power to make better choices. But the difficulty with this view is that the real human problem which makes a hell of so large a part of man's life is to be found in those choices in which men are partly self-deceived. If they were wholly self-deceived there would be no freedom and hence no sin. Also it seems impossible to separate in practice the factor of self-deception from the factor of deliberate choice of evil." [2]

But the real question is not what factors we can separate

[1] *Liberal Theology*, edited by D. E. Roberts and H. Van Dusan, p. 191.

[2] *Op. cit.*, p. 199.

in practice, but what is the significance of those factors for theoretical analysis.

We are also invited by Bennett to a repentance, not merely for "the guilt for evil of which one is clearly the cause,"[1] but also for "that kind of solidarity that one may feel with the sin of the nation" and because "the best that is possible involves participation in evils that harass the conscience."[2] Nor is this a mere discipline. It has a rationale, apparently, in final theological truth.

Accommodations of this kind are fatal. If liberalism is to play its part in the quickening of a religious awareness that will not be out of harmony with the genuine intellectual and cultural advances of our time—and there can be no more urgent task—it must be by laying hold more firmly than ever on the principle that the individual is responsible, in the proper moral and religious sense, only for deliberate betrayal of his ideals, and by thinking out afresh the implications of this principle and relating it to the religious life as a whole.

With the more positive side of this task we are not much concerned at present. But some observations upon it, in the next chapter, may help us to set our main arguments in their proper setting.

[1] *Op. cit.*, p. 202.　　　　[2] *Op. cit.*, p. 203.

CHAPTER XII

REVELATION AND MORALS

I F T H E A I M W E H A V E just described is to be achieved there must be acquired a new sense of reality. Mankind has become obsessed with its own attainments, and is living overmuch on the resources of its own mind. The conquest of nature is apt, for this reason, to be very delusive; for, while understanding and control are extended in remarkable ways, the mystery eludes us. The communion with things has been broken, and we find ourselves left with an empty husk, a form without substance. In so far as liberalism and humanism have aided this alienation of man from his environment, in so far as they have helped to drive him into the ivory towers of his thought, they have merited much of the abuse which they have received so abundantly of late. Reference was made above to the proneness of liberalism to identify itself with prevailing trends. The main factors in the progress of man since the fifteenth century have been the greater sway of the intellect and the emancipation of the individual—still, incidentally, far from coming to his own. Religious liberalism has played its part here, a very noble part in many regards, but it has also helped to induce the debilitating preoccupation of man with himself. Our attainments are real enough, they are most valuable, and they will no doubt be extended in the future very rapidly and in ways that can hardly be comprehended at present. To oppose them, to pick a stupid quarrel with science, is vain reaction. Men will not find easement by creeping back into the lives of their ancestors. It is not at the level of crude primitive contacts that we must seek out reality to-day. We must continue to grow as we have begun, but the time has also come now to bend back our powers and achievements into closer contact with reality in that aspect of it which cannot be subdued by our thought or made amenable to our will. This is the real crisis of our age. If it is surmounted, if reality in its uniqueness and immediacy breaks afresh upon the mind at its present level of attainment, if enlightenment is matched by revelation, there may be such a heightening of perception, such a new power of life, as may take mankind over into something very like a new dimension.

In so far as it expresses such a need, and helps to mediate that which will supply it, the New Theology, with its strong apocalyptic strain, its emphasis on crisis and existential thinking and on the wholly 'other' character of God, is prophetic indeed. If regarded symbolically rather than as literal doctrine, and if purged of the elements of reaction with which its insights are confused, it has a tremendous relevance to our times, and may prove the most important harbinger of a new day.

Art is in very like case to religion, and reflection upon the crisis in art, and especially in poetry, to-day will help us to read aright the riddle of our times. For art is also a revelation of reality, and not, as is so commonly supposed in æsthetic theory, the expression of emotion. The emotion is secondary and derivative. It is what the artist sees that comes first, and his seeing is of a peculiar kind that will not admit of rational description. Science and poetry are poles apart, for the poet brings reality home to us in its individual and immediate aspect by suggestion and symbol. He makes us aware of the familiar in a new way, so that he leaves us breathless with wonder that anything should be what it is. But a revelation of this kind must take us by surprise, it must always be novel. And for that reason poetry becomes harder in every age, many of the ways of taking ourselves artistically by surprise being exhausted. Some artists seek this novelty in new forms and structures. But that in itself is a vain expedient and makes art dilettante and artificial. For the poetic symbol cannot be abstracted from what it expresses, there are no artistic forms waiting to be appropriated and suited to some purpose of the artist. But neither is there some specific artistic content, some new material, that will serve our turn. It is not the newness of a theme that will make for new poetry. Failure to appreciate these correlative principles makes for much obscurantism, on the one hand, and triteness, on the other, in modern poetry. The need is for a new way to be aware of reality, and this is strikingly achieved in some recent poetry where the writer hits on symbols that make the world articulate as never before. It is for lack of such vision that peoples perish and become, as one of the finest of our poets puts it, 'hollow men,' 'stuffed men,' inhabitants of a Waste Land. But where the vision is attained, it is as the opening of a gateway into an entirely new land, a land more wonderful than dreams, for its magic does not evaporate before the fullness of our powers. And this analogy of art with religion is really more than an analogy.[1] For all revelation is ultimately a revelation of God.

It seems, therefore, not idle to hope that the emphasis on the transcendent character of religion in recent Protestant thought will eventually be seen in a new light, and that its role will be entirely changed. Instead of presenting harsh opposition to enlightened ethical thought, and providing the rallying point for desperate reactionary forces, it may itself be the means of so transmuting the main concerns of men as to draw

[1] I have discussed this topic more fully in my paper 'On Poetic Truth,' *Philosophy*, July, 1946.

them into a religious wholeness of life not possible at an earlier stage of civilization. This will bring society out of its present alternation of despair and feverish ill-directed activity, and set it astir with new perceptions, a new power of life; there will be a new and profound sense of expectancy and wonder, disturbing but sobering too.

To discuss the prospect of this religious regeneration of a world distraught is not to the purpose here. But we have to touch on one aspect of the matter which bears very closely on our main theme.

For morality, when its autonomy is unimpaired, presents a unique form of that discipline by which the individual is made to turn his mind outward from himself and becomes more aware of realities which cannot be dissolved into the categories of his thought or made amenable to his will. Vicissitudes and sorrows also play an important part here. So do those limitations of aim which are forced upon us by the passage of years. The growth of character depends largely on a deepening awareness of the inevitability by which things are what they are. But this fashioning of a self through the impact of reality upon it takes a special form in ethics. In the first place, we have here the discipline of values, not of facts. Secondly, in properly moral activities we are confronted with a claim that is entirely outside ourselves in a way that has no parallel in other spheres of value. For although the values of truth or of beauty or of the natural perfection of character are objective in the sense that they do not depend on our reactions or feelings, the attainment of them is not possible unless our interest in the objects or activities that possess them is aroused. No one could write poetry without enthusiasm or appreciate it without being deeply stirred. The pursuit of knowledge could hardly reach the level of new discoveries and apprehensions without intense intellectual curiosity.

There could be no benevolence without spontaneity, no holiness without love. In each of these cases the end to be attained must find lodgment in our own hearts, it must be absorbed into the deepest levels of our own life. But these conditions are reversed in the case of moral effort. For here we are required to respond to ends which stand in the starkness of their claim upon us. And, except when we allow the conscience to become blunted by indifference and turpitude, properly moral activities keep us acutely conscious of a reality not ourselves, the soul remains attuned to what is outside, and there is ensured greater receptivity and sanity in all its responses. The unique realism of morality thus gives it a distinctive function in the growth and maintenance of the true life of the soul.

From this it will be evident that a realist ethic, and especially one which ascribes the central position to the confrontation of the individual by a duty not constituted in any way by his own nature or inclination, a demand altogether outside himself which burns inexorably into his consciousness, has a very important point of contact with religious views which turn on the invasion of human life by a reality overwhelmingly greater and other than ourselves.

In the true interest of the transcendentalist doctrines themselves, it is, therefore, essential to preserve the autonomy of morals. It will be recalled how the latter was conceived. Morality as we presented it above is very complete and self-contained. Moral worth depends solely on the response of the individual. And, while that response presupposes a system of objective duties not always coincident with the duty that the agent presents to himself and in terms of his loyalty to which moral worth must be appraised, the existence of that system of duties is apprehended as an ultimate ethical truth not requiring support from any other source. The assumption that ethics depends on some metaphysical or religious principle leads, as was also indicated, to those distortions of ethical truths which we have set ourselves especially to counter in this book. The absorption of ethics in religion must be steadily resisted. But we can now see more clearly that this is as much in the interest of religion as of ethics. We are not committed to the view that ethics and religion have no very close relation. It is plain in fact that they have. No experience requires a universe to itself in order to be unique, and the closeness of the relation between ethics and religion is too evident to need stressing. It is exhibited alike in the obvious superiority of the more completely moralized religions and in the history of ethical enlightenment. The piety which is contemptuous of 'works' is immediately suspect. But all this is just what we should expect when we reflect on the implications of moral autonomy for the life of the spirit as a whole.

This requires to be stressed in reinforcement of what was said in an earlier chapter regarding the danger to religion as well as to moral and political activities of an isolation of religion from the moral life of the individual.

It should be added that the view we take of the moral life and its function in no way precludes the emphasis that also falls to be placed upon the disastrous effect for human life as a whole, whether we think of the individual or of society, of an alienation of man from God. If man has the capacity of knowing God and enjoying him, there can be nothing but the direst frustrations, the most maddening when least understood, when the capacity goes unfulfilled. Bewilderment, cynicism, and disorder are inevitable. Man created in the image of God cannot set his house in order without God; if the house is empty, however carefully the scientist may sweep and garnish it, the 'devils' will return and make our state 'worse than before.' In stressing this the theological thinker requires no curb, and it was to a religious experience of a newer and finer kind than has been known hitherto that we ourselves bade the reader look for the hope of a regenerated world. But here we have also to remember that life as a whole is more than morality, and that disasters of a quite overwhelming kind may come about in ways that are not primarily ethical. Man needs to win moral battles, but he also needs to learn wisdom and to acquire graciousness and religious sensitivity. And in the context of success or failure in these regards the language of religious or theological thought may retain a terrible significance in some ways which have no direct relation to the moral field. By throwing man, in respect to his moral activities, entirely upon his own resources, we must not be taken to ignore other needs, equally fundamental in the economy of his life as a whole, which man cannot supply in the same fashion for himself.

Neither do these considerations imply that the idea of salvation must be shifted to another sphere than that of moral struggles, successes, failures. The truth here is, I think, quite simple. It is the whole man that must be saved, or, to put it, I think better, the need of man is to be made whole, and this will include redeeming him from the 'penalty of sin.' It will include this above all, for it is here that man feels his failure most acutely. But the issues that arise here are considerably simplified on the view taken in this essay of the nature of morality and its relation to religion; and the latter view therefore takes us deeper into the heart of this tremendous problem of salvation than any other.

It is with this matter that I should like to close, bringing the reader nearer to celebrated Christian doctrines than he probably ever hoped to come. Our view of the relation of morality to the transcendent character of religion, with its stress on the educative function of the unique realism of morals, will, I suggest, help us, on the one hand, to understand the peculiar sense of sublimity and elation which goes with the true moral triumph—true as distinct from the smug and spurious sense of righteousness which has not been preceded by a real struggle with ourselves and does not humble the heart. It will also show us, on the other hand, how failure brings a distinctive feeling of an impoverishing of life, the sense that we have abrogated the means of nurturing the self, the despair that goes with remorse because of a cutting of ourselves from the universe that sustains us—by all of which we come to speak of death as the 'penalty of sin.' Into the implications of this penalty we cannot enquire closely. It is easy to describe it crudely, even when we are free of doctrinal presumptions, for the experience of devastating loneliness which follows the alienation of self from reality in sin, cannot be easily compressed into formulæ. But it can be seen how close we come here to a supreme religious need, the need for salvation by making the entry of the Divine into human life possible when that life is turned inward and deprived of the sense of reality. Can we not in these ways discover the true significance of the supreme experiences of religion, 'conversion,' 'atonement,' 'new birth,' 'salvation'? I suggest that we can; and without pursuing the matter here, it may be stressed that we need all the more, for that reason, to lay hold very firmly of the principles of moral objectivity and autonomy. For in addition to their inherent importance, they seem to provide also the clue to the new synthesis in religious thinking of which we stand in such need. They will do this, we must repeat, when the ultimacy of ethical truths, for finite thought, is clearly perceived, when ethics, as Kant said of the good will, is made to shine like a jewel by its own light—then, *and then only*.

INDEX OF PROPER NAMES